Books are to be returned on or before
the last date below.

THE

Ritz

LONDON BOOK OF

Christmas

THE

Ritz

LONDON BOOK OF

Christmas

JENNIE REEKIE

Ebury Press
LONDON

3 5 7 9 10 8 6 4

Published in 2007 by Ebury Press, an imprint of Ebury Publishing

A Random House Group Company

Copyright © The Random Century Group 1989

The Random House Group Limited Reg. No. 954009

Addresses for companies within the Random House Group can be found at
www.randomhouse.co.uk

A CIP catalogue record for this book is available from the British Library

The Random House Group Limited makes every effort to ensure that the papers used in our books are made from trees that have been legally sourced from well-managed and credibly certified forests. Our paper procurement policy can be found on
www.randomhouse.co.uk

To buy books by your favourite authors and register for offers visit
www.rbooks.co.uk

Printed and bound at TienWah Press in Singapore

ISBN 9780852237441

Editor: Sue Carpenter
Designer: Peartree Design Associates
Illustrators: Dennis and Sheila Curran

Acknowledgements

The author would like to thank Terry Holme Roger Ellis and Bob Burton of The Ritz Hotel London for their help.

The publishers would like to thank the following for permission to reprint copyright material:

Page 15 Reprinted by permission of John Murray (Publishers) Ltd from *Collected Poem* by Sir John Betjeman

Page 29 Reprinted by permission of Cambridge University Press from *Selected Letters*, D. H Lawrence

Page 30 Reprinted by permission of Faber and Faber Ltd from *The Country Child* by Alison Uttley

As well as giving recipes for Christmas dishes served at The Ritz Hotel, London this book includes many additional ideas. The hotel does not serve all the dishes for which recipe are given here.

Note on flour for those using Cup Measures All-purpose flour can be substituted for cake flour, although this may not give such fine results.

Contents

Christmas at the Ritz

The London Ritz opened on the 15th May 1906, in an era when Christmas and its festivities were being enjoyed to the full. Victorian society, aided and abetted by Charles Dickens and the royal family had, in a wave of nostalgia, regenerated this religious feast, and made it the most important time of the year. With their love of tradition I they took the best of the old and combined it with the new to make Christmas into a happy and joyous occasion, and one that was essentially family, orientated.

To spend Christmas at the Ritz today is to take a step back in time -to a golden age of luxury,

elegance, service and style. The atmosphere that of a large house party at which th Edwardian society of Edward VI, Lily Langtr and Alice Keppel, who graced the hotel when first opened, would have felt entirely at home.

From the week before Chris mas, when in the evenir a choir sings carols i the Palm Court, th true spirit Christmas is ca tured and pe vades every co ner of the hote The publ rooms, such the Palm Cou and the Dinnir room are fab lously decorate with a differe theme every year. th suites all have their ow

Christmas tree so that families can put their pres-
nts round their own tree and feel truly 'at
ome'. Lighted trees line the Long Gallery
which leads from the dining room to the rotunda
r main entrance hall, where, by the porter's desk
45 ft Christmas tree stands majestically,
dorned with hundreds of lights and Victorian
ecorations.

The exact way in which the three days are cel-
brated varies from time to time. When this book
was first published in 1988 there was a christmas
package which was a true gala occasion. For
hose staying in the hotel for the Christmas
reak, the festivities start with a reception on
Christmas Eve in the Marie Antoinette Suite–a
rivate room exquisitely decorated and furnished
n the style of Louis XVI–to the accompaniment
f the choir.

Interesting cocktails especially created for the
ccasion by the head barman, together with an
ppetizing array of canapés and cocktail snacks
ets the tone for the next three days. Later in the
vening, many walk to midnight mass at one of
he historic churches in St James's and are then
velcomed back into the warmth with steaming
ot toddies and roast chestnuts, fresh off a street
endor's brazier.

Christmas morning would not be Christmas
norning without stockings and it need hardly be
aid that a Ritz stocking–delivered to every guest
ourtesy of the management–is no mean affair.
Once breakfast has been leisurely disposed of
ere comes the dilemma of whether to opt for
Christmas lunch or dinner, few of today's guests
aving the constitution of their forefathers to
ackle both!

THE HOLLY AND THE IVY . . .

The damsel donned her kirtle sheen,
The hall was decked with holly green
Forth to the woods did merry men go
To gather in the mistletoe

Marmion, Sir Walter Scott

César Ritz, founder of the Ritz hotels, with
justly deserved pride, described the diningroom
of the Ritz as 'one of the loveliest rooms in the
world'. From one end, the figures of Neptune
and one of his nereids preside over a room of
sumptuous beauty in which have dined kings
and queens, heads of state, aristocrats, socialites,
bishops and actresses. What better setting could
there be for enjoying such a celebrated British
institution as Christmas lunch or dinner? ...
Perfectly cooked roast goose with ambrosial stuffing and apple sauce, or succulent Norfolk turkey,
bread and cranberry sauces, crisp roast potatoes,
delicate roast parsnips, bright green Brussels
sprouts; followed by well matured Christmas
pudding laced with brandy, and delectable mince
pies topped with rich brandy butter. To end the
repast, perhaps a little helping of Stilton, Bath
Olivers and celery, accompanied by a glass of port
from the excellent wine cellar? Crackers, hats
and party poppers all add to the infectious gaiety
of a day like no other.

Once all the guests have finished eating lunch,
it is the turn of the. staff to enjoy their Christmas
meal. Following a tradition which dates back to
the Roman feast of Saturnalia, when masters
waited upon their slaves, the management wait
upon the staff. The food is the same as that
served in the dining-room, the atmosphere per-

haps even more exuberant, as those who have been working since dawn finally relax and enjoy themselves.

oxing Day

For those who feel that some fresh air is essential on Boxing Day, a luxury coach leaves the hotel after breakfast, bound for Kempton Park Races. The amount of exercise involved in the walk from the stand to the paddock or the bookies' may be nominal, but it will make you feel more virtuous. The feature race, the King George V steeplechase, is one of the highlights of the racing calendar and always attracts a high-class international field of horses, so, win or lose, it is a worthy spectacle. A magnificent champagne picnic and atten-

dant waiters accompany the coach, so there are no worries about having to fight one's way through overcrowded bars to obtain a drink. There are even some 'racegers', who find it unnecessary to leave the warmth and comfort of the coach all day!

The evening is an opportunity either to drown sorrows over losses or celebrate winnings in style at a Gala Dinner Dance. Champagne cocktails are followed by a gourmet dinner devised by the head chef, Sitting in the dining-room beneath the painted *trompe-l'oeil* ceiling, the candelabra.glittering and live music of the Twenties and Thirties floating through the air, it is all too easy to be lulled into believing that those halcyon years of grace and elegance have returned for ever.

THE HISTORY OF BOXING DAY

Boxing Day takes its name from alms boxes placed outside churches during the Christmas period, which were opened on the 26th, when collecting ceased, and the contents distributed among the poor.

The 'box' used was an earthenware pot with a simple slit in the top, so that it had to be broken open with a hammer to retrieve the money. A similar box was used by apprentices and servants who were allowed to ask their master and his friends for money during Advent. The obvious advantage of this type of box was that it was impossible to rifle before the due date. It was described in 1611 as 'a box having a cleft on the lid, or in the side, for money to enter it; used in

France by begging Fryers and here by Butlers, and Prentices etc.'

From around the eighteenth century, the expression 'Christmas Box' was also used for gifts of money given to servants and to tradespeople who had provided a service during the year. This practice is not as widespread as it was a few years ago, but there are still some people such as postmen, milkmen and paper boys who expect a Christmas Box— and woe betide you should you for- get the dustmen!

The Customs of Christmas Past

The birthday of Jesus is celebrated throughout Christendom on 25th December, but the origins of this Christian festival are purely pagan. No one knows with any certainty the exact day Christ was born (indeed it is now thought more than likely that it was summer, especially as it would have been unusual for shepherds to be watching their flocks by night in Palestine in the middle of December!), but in the fourth century it was suggested to Pope Julius I that 25th December could be the day.

It delighted him as it roughly coincided with a number of pagan feasts, including the Roman ones of Saturnalia (dedicated to the god Saturn) from 17–23rd December and the Birthday of the Unconquered Sun on the 25th, as well as the northern European winter solstice festivities, also known as the Festival of Yule, which started on 21st December and lasted several weeks. Unable to eliminate these pagan feasts, the church wished to absorb them into the Christian faith, and this seemed the ideal opportunity. Pope Julius therefore decreed that 25th December *was* Christ's birthday— and so it has remained for the last 15 centuries.

The most obvious pagan relic in northern Europe is the decorating of houses with evergreens, a practice which can be traced back over 2,000 years to the Druids who would adorn their dwellings and sacred places in this manner. Holly, ivy and mistletoe were all considered to be magical plants because they not only retained their leaves in winter, but also bore fruit at this time. New teachings were cleverly introduced by the clergy; in the sixth century, Pope Gregory I advised Augustine, the first Archbishop of Canterbury, to encourage any local customs which were capable of Christian interpretation. By the Middle Ages holly berries had come to symbolize the blood of Christ, the prickly leaves—the crown of thorns, and clinging ivy—immortality.

Both holly and ivy were used for decorating churches as well as homes, but mistletoe, which had been worshipped by the Druids, was considered too pagan and sinful to be allowed to enter any hallowed portals. Indeed its presence is still forbidden in most churches today, th one exception being York Minster. Here, fo lowing a medieval ritual, a branch is placed o the high altar on Christmas Eve and remain there until the Feast of the Epiphany on 6t January.

While decorating with evergreens is commo throughout northern Europe, the custom c kissing under the mistletoe is purely Englisł Before the advent of the Christmas tree, a cir cular evergreen bough, known as the kissin bough, would be brought into the house or Christmas Eve. (Until recently it was considere very unlucky to put up any form of decoratio before the 24th.) It would be festooned wit candles, red apples, paper decorations, orna ments, and a large bunch of mistletoe. Any gir standing under this was entitled to claim a kiss In some parts of England the man was allowe to kiss the girl as many times as there wer berries in the bunch—which in prolific year doubtless resulted in passionate embraces!

The Cattle are Lowing...

Throughout Europe it was widely believed that at midnight on Christmas Eve, all the farmyard animals knelt down in reverence to the Christ child and spoke in human tongues. Bees were also said to wake from hibernation and sing the 100th psalm.

It may seem strange that people did not sit up with the animals in an attempt to witness the sight, but perhaps it was because, as Thomas Hardy wrote, everyone wanted it to be true.

Good Tidings We Bring...

Carols came from France round about 1300 and at one time were sung at all the feast days during the year: Easter, Whitsun, May Day, etc., as well as Christmas. The word originates from the French *carole* meaning ring, as early carollers would dance around in a ring as they sang.

Some of these carols had a religious significance, but in a volume published in 1550, the greater majority were ballads of the kind minstrels sang at feasts and banquets. Their use at such occasions went on into the next century and in 1626 one Michael Breton wrote, 'not a cup of drink must pass without a carol'.

In England, during the puritanical regime of Oliver Cromwell in the mid-seventeenth century, celebrations for Christmas Day were abolished. Shops had to stay open, churches were locked and anyone (priests included) found celebrating the Nativity was imprisoned. The only kind of carols permitted were dull dirges

'Christmas Eve and twelve o'clock
Now they are all on their knees,'
An elder said as we sat in a flock
By the embers in fireside ease.

We pictured the meek mild creatures, where
They dwelt in their strawy pen,
Nor did it occur to one of us there
To doubt they were kneeling then.

So fair a fancy would weave
In these years! Yet I feel
If someone said on Christmas Eve
'Come; see the oxen kneel

In the lonely barton by yonder coomb,
Our children used to know'
I should go with him in the gloom
Hoping it might be so.

The Oxen, Thomas Hardy

which had little of the 'tidings of comfort and joy' of their predecessors.

Following the restoration of the monarchy in 1660, Christmas became a joyous occasion once again, but the tradition of singing carols lapsed, apart from in a few country areas, until it was revived by the Victorians in the middle of the nineteenth century. With their desire to re-create Christmas as they felt it used to be in the good old days before Cromwell's Protectorate, they collected old carols and Christmas hymns, wrote new ones and published countless volumes.

By the 1880s it had become popular to sing carols in church, as well as in the street, where bands of children would go from house to house singing, often being rewarded with mince pies and a warming drink. Christmas cards were illustrated with pictures of people standing with a lantern, or by a gas lamp, well wrapped up with mufflers and hats against the cold. A piano was still to be found in every living-room, be it a grand in an elegant drawing-room, or a small upright in a front parlour. On Christmas Eve many families would gather round the tree to sing carols, with mother or one of the daughters accompanying on the piano.

'Today I have two children of my own to give presents to, who, they know not why, are full of happy wonder at the German Christmas tree and its radiant candles.'

Queen Victoria, 1841

We Wish You A Merry Christmas...

The sending of Christmas cards is a comparatively recent custom as the first cards were not produced until 1843. In the eighteenth and early nineteenth century it had been common practice among close friends and relations to send a 'Christmas piece'. This would consist of a few lines usually written on specially prepared sheets, decorated with borders and scrolls.

In 1843 Sir Henry Cole, the man responsible for making the sketch from which the first postage stamp—the Penny Black—was engraved, suggested the idea of a card to Royal Academician John Horsley. Horsley thus designed the first Christmas card, and about 1,000 were sold from Felix Summerly's Home Treasury at 12 Old Bond Street.

The availability of the penny post and improved printing techniques, enabling cards to be produced more cheaply, gave the embryonic industry the boost it needed and by 1880 cards had become an established part of the Christmas festivities. Initially the designs had little religious connection (Horsley's original card showed three generations of a family quaffing wine), but this element gradually increased towards the end of the century. Holly and mistletoe were popular themes from as early as 1862, as were snow and the robin, who was always considered a firm friend of man and the symbol of life-giving fire. One of the many explanations for the robin's red breast was that, on the night of the Nativity, he had fanned the infant Jesus with his wings to spread the warmth of a brazier but in doing so had burnt his chest.

O Christmas Tree, O Christmas Tree . . .

Queen Victoria's Consort may not have the reputation of being the life and soul of the party, but Christmas, being family-orientated, was a celebration he enjoyed. In 1841, the Prince Consort imported a Christmas tree to Windsor Castle from his native Germany so that his family could enjoy what had been one of the great delights of his own childhood. Adorned with gilded fruits and nuts, sweets and paper roses in the German manner, and with the miniature candles throwing out their enchanting soft light, it is not surprising it was an instant success in the royal household.

A few Christmas trees had been seen earlier in England. It is recorded that there was one at a children's party given by Queen Caroline in 1820, and German settlers to the north of England at the beginning of the century had started the custom there. William Howitt recorded this in 1840 when he wrote in *The Rural Life of England* that the idea was 'spreading fast

among the English there'. But it was the royal tree that really started the fashion since anything the royal family did was quickly emulated by their subjects. In 1848 a picture appeared in *The Illustrated London News* of the Queen and Prince with their children around a lighted tree. It had been given not only royal consent, but approval. Charles Dickens may have considered it a 'new German toy' in 1850, but within 20 years it had become *de rigueur* in most households.

Today the Christmas tree is to be found in almost every home, church, central town square and village green. To every young child it is the focal point of Christmas in their home, and nothing can diminish their excitement the day it is erected, even if replacing the candles with coloured electric bulbs—though expedient and safer—has destroyed just a *little* of the romance of the tree.

The best-known and most spectacular tree must be the one erected in Trafalgar Square each year. Presented annually by the people of Oslo to the people of London since 1947, it is scarcely shorter than Nelson's Column and always breathtakingly illuminated. At St Paul's Cathedral, both the tree in the portico and the one inside the West Door are donated by the Queen from her estates, while The Ritz turns to the original source of the Christmas tree—Germany—for the impressive 45 ft specimen in the rotunda.

'In the middle of the table was a Christmas tree, alive and growing, looking very much surprised at itself, for had not Tom dug it up from the plantation whilst they were at church, and brought it in with real snow on its branches? The rosiest of apples and the nicest yellow oranges were strung to its boughs, and some sugar biscuits with pink icing and a few humbugs from Tom's pocket lay on the snow, with a couple of gaily coloured texts and a sugar elephant. On the top of the tree shone a silver bird, a most astonishing silver glass peacock with a tail of fine feathers, which might have flown in at the window.'

The Country Child, Alison Uttley

A WISH.

Let joy or ease, let affluence or content,
And the gay conscience of a life well spent,
Calm every thought, in spirit every grace,
Glow in thy heart and smile upon thy face.

$\mathcal{B}$earing Gifts We Traverse Afar . . .

Exchanging gifts at Christmas time can be traced back to the ancient Roman tradition of giving presents to their Emperor on New Year's Day. Usually a voluntary gesture of respect, Caligula took it one step further and *demanded* his officials bring him presents, while he stood on the steps of his palace to receive them.

In the southern European countries such as Italy, Spain and even France, it became customary to exchange gifts on Twelfth Night in commemoration of the visit of the Three Kings, but in Britain until the mid-nineteenth century, presents were given on New Year's Day.

The change to Christmas Day took place gradually, over 20 or 30 years. Certainly it had not occurred by 1844 when Dickens, one of the most cognizant people of his time on the subject of Christmas customs, wrote in *The Chimes*, 'The streets were full of motion, and the shops were decked out gaily. The New Year, like an infant Heir to the whole world, was waited for, with welcomes, presents and rejoicings'; and no mention is made of presents on Christmas Day in *A Christmas Carol*.

Until this century, Christmas gifts were not expensive extravaganzas, but more modest tokens: fruit and small toys for children, works of art and needlework samplers from children to parents and almanacs between adults.

. . . The holly in the windy hedge
And round the Manor House the yew
Will soon be stripped to deck the ledge,
The altar, font and arch and pew
So that the villagers can say
'The church looks nice' on Christmas Day . . .

. . . And is it true? And is it true,
This most tremendous tale of all,
Seen in a stained-glass window's hue,
A Baby in an ox's stall?
The Maker of the stars and sea
Become a Child on earth for me?

And is it true? For if it is,
No loving fingers tying strings
Around those tissued fripperies,
The sweet and silly Christmas things,
Bath salts and inexpensive scent
And hideous tie so kindly meant,

No love that in a family dwells,
No carolling in frosty air,
Nor all the steeple-shaking bells
Can with this single Truth compare—
That God was Man in Palestine
And lives today in Bread and Wine.

Christmas, Sir John Betjeman, 1954

The Twelve Days of Christmas

The winter solstice festivities used to last for several weeks and so the early church decreed in the sixth-century that the festival of Christmas should span from Christmas Day through to the Feast of the Epiphany on 6th January. The Saxon king, Alfred (of burnt cakes fame), went to great pains to ensure this teaching of the church was carried out and forbade any work to be done during this period. Legend has it that this instruction cost him the Battle of Chippenham in 878 to the Danes, as he refused to fight during the twelve days of Christmas.

In the reign of Henry VIII, the ordinary working people were encouraged to play games over Christmas since a proclamation forbade them to do so at any other time: 'Artificer, or Craftsman of any handicraft or occupation, Husbandman, Apprentice, Labourer, Servant at husbandry... [must not]...play at Tables, Tennis, Dice, Cards, Bowls, Clash, Coyting, Logating or any other unlawful game, out of Christmas, as under pain of twenty shillings to be forfeit for every time....

According to a sixteenth-century writer, Christmas was a time for 'carols, wassailing bowl, dancing' and the playing of games such as 'about May pole, shoeing the wild horse, hoodman blind, and hot cockles

Boxing Day

The first of the twelve days was not, as one might expect, Christmas, but Boxing Day or the Feast of St Stephen. There were in fact two St Stephens, and over the centuries the distinction between them blurred and the first St Stephen took on the mantle of the second. The original St Stephen, whose saint's day it is, became the first Christian martyr when he was stoned to death in AD 33. The second was a ninth-century Swedish missionary who, for obscure reasons, was associated with horses.

The result is that in medieval England, horses were bled on this day, which, it was felt, improved their general health, but doubtless sent a few to an early grave! Throughout Europe various horse-blessing ceremonies were performed, and this may explain why St Stephen's Day has for so long been associated with hunting, racing and other outdoor sports and their attendant food.

'The wren the king of all the birds
Was caught on St Stephen's Day
in the furze.'

Hunting the Wren was a traditional, somewhat macabre sport, always carried out on St Stephen's Day. As the Druids sat around the fires they burnt to aid the ailing sun at their winter feast, they desired to know what the future held, and it was said this could be prophesied from the song of a wren—but first it had to be captured. The origins of this practice were soon lost in the mists of time, but the wren continued to be hunted until the beginning of this century. Once caught, it was put into a 'wren house' which frequently took the form of a stable lantern, and was paraded through the streets with much rejoicing. Sadly, as a culmination to the festivities, it was often, though not always, killed.

Holy Innocent's or Childermas Day (28th December)

This festival commemorates the massacre of the innocent children by Herod. In France and Italy this day was also known as the Feast of Fools and the Feast of Asses, when people brayed the

> On the first day of Christmas
> My true love gave to me
> A partridge in a pear tree ...
>
> On the twelfth day of Christmas
> My true love gave to me
> Twelve drummers drumming
> Eleven pipers piping
> Ten lords a-leaping
> Nine ladies dancing
> Eight maids a-milking
> Seven swans a-swimming
> Six geese a-laying
> Five gold rings
> Four calling birds
> Three French hens
> Two turtle doves
> And a partridge in a pear tree
>
> Anon

responses at Mass. In England, from the thirteenth to the seventeenth century, it was the day of the 'boy bishop'. A young chorister would be dressed in bishop's robes and would be allowed to perform mass before processing through the streets with his retinue and being showered with sweetmeats and coins.

New Year's Eve and New Year's Day

Though celebrated in England and Wales, New Year's Eve is when the Scots really come into their own. With a puritanical streak always running through their veins, they took the restrictions imposed by Cromwell to heart, and since that time Christmas has never regained its former eminence in the Scottish calendar. New Year—or Hogmanay—became, and remained the night for major winter celebration.

One old Highland practice consisted of someone donning the hide of a cow and being chased through the streets by other villagers. He would then knock on the door of a house and plead to be let in, whereupon he and his pursuers would be offered food and drink, in return for which

THE ROYAL EPIPHANY GIFTS

To commemorate the gifts of the Three Kings, since the eleventh century a ceremony takes place each year on the Feast of the Epiphany at which the reigning monarch presents gold, frankincense and myrrh at the altar. The sovereign always made the offering in person until George III was too mad to perform this or any other public duty, and since then it has always been done by proxy.

Other chapels were used previously, but now the ceremony takes place at 11.30 a.m. in the Chapel Royal at St James's Palace. During the offertory the Gentlemen of the Chapel Royal, representing the monarch, place the gifts in silk purses on a silver alms salver and

carry them to the altar rails to be blessed by the priest. The incenses, frankincense and myrrh, have little intrinsic value, but the gold, which consists of 25 sovereigns, is distributed among charities for the aged poor.

he householders would strip off a small portion of the hide for good luck.

A similar—though probably unconnected—practice, customary in the north of England as well as Scotland, is first-footing. As soon as the clock has struck midnight, people wait in anticipation and trepidation for a knock on their door to see who will be the first person—or first-footer—to cross their threshold. Ideally it will be a tall, dark, handsome man bringing with him gifts of coal, bread, salt or whisky; if he is a stranger, so much the better, for this is a further propitious sign. The worst thing that can possibly happen is for a woman to darken your door, for then the year ahead will be an unmitigated disaster.

*T*welfth Night

Christmas goes out in fine style—with Twelfth Night. It is a finish worthy of the time. Christmas Day was the morning of the season; New Year's Day the middle of it or noon; Twelfth Night is the night, brilliant with innumerable planets of Twelfth Cakes.' So wrote the essayist James Henry Leigh Hunt in 1840, and until the middle of the nineteenth century, Twelfth Night was the exuberant Christmas finale—the feast to end all feasts.

The festivities centred around the Twelfth-Night Cake (see page 43) in which, before it was baked, were buried a bean and a pea. The man who found the bean became the King for the evening and the woman who discovered the pea, the Queen. Should a man find the pea, then he was entitled to choose his Queen from the assembled company, while if a woman found the bean, she could choose her King.

Once the King and Queen had been established, the evening's revelry would begin in earnest. Games, such as forfeits, disguisings and play-acting were common, and by the beginning of the nineteenth century, charades and snapdragon were added to the list. In medieval England, Twelfth Night marked the last day of the reign of the Lord of Misrule, who would have presided over the fun and games of the preceding eleven days, assisted by a loyal band of courtiers, all suitably ridiculously attired.

While some left their decorations up until Candlemas on the 2nd February, most people took them down on Twelfth Night, for if left longer every holly leaf and sprig of berries turned into mischievous spirits. It was considered equally unlucky to take the decorations down earlier—customs which many people are still as conscious and conscientious about today.

NEW YEAR'S EVE AT THE RITZ

Tall, dark, handsome strangers clutching pieces of coal do not walk into the Ritz dining room as soon as the chimes of Big Ben have faded away, but a piper in full Scottish regalia does, as balloons cascade from the ceiling and fireworks explode in the garden outside. The New Year is welcomed in in style and anyone who has the opportunity of trying it once—together with the elaborate seven-course dinner, band and cabaret—does so again and again and again.

Hot Soup

Soup is essential at that great Boxing Day institution, the shooting lunch. Prior to the invention of vacuum flasks, it would have been taken out to the guns, beaters and other followers in a 'hay box', a large wooden box lined with newspaper and filled with hay. The vessel containing the soup would be placed in the middle and more hay packed around it for insulation.

There is always a plentiful supply of good stock from the turkey to make the base of a flavoursome soup.

CELERIAC AND STILTON SOUP

METRIC/IMPERIAL	CUP MEASURES
50 g/2 oz butter	¼ cup butter
2 leeks, trimmed, washed and roughly chopped	2 medium leeks, trimmed, washed and roughly chopped
juice of 1 lemon	juice of 1 lemon
2 celeriac, total weight about 900 g/2 lb	2 lb celery root
1.7 litres/3 pints turkey stock	7½ cups turkey stock
10 ml/2 tsp rubbed fresh sage or 5 ml/1 tsp dried	2 tsp rubbed fresh sage or 1 tsp dried
salt and freshly ground pepper	salt and freshly ground pepper
225 g/8 oz Blue Stilton, rinded and roughly chopped	8 oz crumbly blue cheese, rinded and roughly chopped
300 ml/½ pint single cream	1¼ cups light cream

Serves 8

Melt the butter in a large saucepan, add the leeks and fry very gently for 10 minutes until softened. Meanwhile, fill a bowl with cold water and add the lemon juice to acidulate it. Peel the celeriac thickly with a sharp knife. Cut into chunks, dropping them into the bowl of acidulated water. Drain the celeriac, then add to the pan of leeks. Fry gently, for a further 10 minutes. Add the stock and bring to the boil, stirring, then add the sage and salt and pepper to taste. Lower the heat, cover and simmer for about 20 minutes or until the celeriac is very soft. Crumble the Stilton cheese into a blender or food processor. Add the soup and work to a smooth purée. (You may have to work in batches, according to the size of your machine.) Return the soup to the rinsed-out pan and stir in the cream. Reheat, stirring, then taste and adjust seasoning.

The Handsome Christmas Ham

Christmas is the one time during the year that many people buy a genuine whole or half ham, rather than a joint of gammon. The difference is this: gammon is the hind leg of the pig which is cured–generally in brine–along with the remainder of the side; ham is also the hind leg, but cut off and cured separately, following age-old methods of either dry-salting or sweet-curing in brine with spices, herbs, brown sugar and treacle. Hams are usually left to mature for several months which improves their flavour considerably.

The best-known British ham is the York ham. It is often said that York ham came about because it took 100 years to build York Minster so there was always a plentiful supply of oak sawdust for smoking; however, if you tell that story in Yorkshire they'll laugh, since the York ham is green or unsmoked! Another renowned ham is Bradenham. Originally from the West country, where it is still produced by a few butchers, the Bradenham is easily recognized by its coal-black skin. Created by Lord Bradenham in 1781, the ham is first dry-salted, then marinated in spices, juniper berries and molasses, before being smoked and left to mature for up to seven months.

Fortunately there are still some local butchers and small independent companies throughout the country producing superb hams cured by the old traditional methods. Not only in York and Bradenham but also regional specialities, such as Suffolk and Cumberland as well as some with their own 'secret' recipe. Many operate a mail order service, so everyone, no matter where they live, can still enjoy as perfect a Christmas ham as their forefathers.

GLAZED HAM

Hams that have been cured in the old-fashioned manner require plenty of soaking before cooking. Put into a large bowl of water for between 24 and 36 hours and change the water three or four times. When baking, rather than boiling, soak for the longer period of time.

Originally, baked hams were wrapped in a flour and water pastry, known as a 'huff paste'. This prevented the ham from drying out in the same way as kitchen foil would.

——METRIC/IMPERIAL—— •	——CUP MEASURES——
1 ham weighing between 5.5–6.4 kg/12–14 lb	1 ham weighing between 12–14 lb
8 cloves	8 cloves
peeled rind of 1 orange	peeled rind of 1 orange
6 juniper berries	6 juniper berries
Glaze	*Glaze*
120 ml/8 tbsp clear honey	8 tbsp clear honey
30 ml/2 tbsp dry mustard	2 tbsp dry mustard
60 ml/4 tbsp ginger wine	4 tbsp ginger wine
cloves	cloves

Oven: 350°F/180°C/Mark 4 then
425°F/220°C/Mark 7
Serves 12–14

Remove the ham from the water and dry well with a cloth. Lay either a piece of heavy-duty foil or a double thickness layer of standard foil on a working surface. Put half the cloves, orange rind and juniper berries in the centre. Lay on the ham then put the remaining cloves, orange rind and juniper berries on top of the ham. Bring round the sides of the foil and close so that the ham is completely enveloped. Place the ham in a large roasting tin, then pour in enough boiling water to come about 5 cm/2 inches up the tin (this prevents the ham from drying).

Calculate the cooking time, allowing 25 minutes to the lb and 25 minutes over, and put into the oven. Thirty minutes before the end of cooking, take the ham out of the oven and increase the oven temperature. Remove the foil, then carefully peel off the skin. Score the fat into diamonds.

Pour off the liquid from the roasting tin (this can be reserved and used as stock for soup). Replace the ham in the tin. Mix together the honey and mustard and stir in the ginger wine. Spoon over the ham. Place a clove in the centre of each diamond, then put the ham into the hot oven. Cook for the remaining 30 minutes, basting frequently with the glaze. Remove from the oven and either serve hot or allow to cool.

Game Pie

While more commonly served these days a picnics, or as part of a cold buffet, game pie wa often eaten at hunt breakfasts as this extrac from *Party-Giving on Every Scale*, 1882, shows:

'These breakfasts are given ... by the maste of hounds, by members of the hunt, or by an country gentleman near whose residence th meet takes place ....

'9.30 to 10 a.m. is the time usually fixed for hunt breakfast ... hot entrées are not given; large supply of cold viands is necessary; col beef is the *pièce de résistance* at these entertair ments, as the hunting farmers prefer somethin substantial to commence upon ....

'Cold roast pheasant or game pie, roast chicke or roast turkey would also be given .... All th cold meats, game, etc., are placed on the break fast table and the guests help themselves ....

'Sherry, brandy, cherry-brandy, liqueurs an ale are always provided. Champagne is onl occasionally given.'

These lavish affairs have now been discarde by all but a few hunts. For those that do carr on the tradition, the hunt breakfast at the Box ing Day and New Year's Day meets something special.

RAISED GAME PIE

METRIC/IMPERIAL	•	CUP MEASURES
1 pheasant		1 pheasant
4 rabbit joints, total weight about 450 g/1 lb		4 rabbit joints, total weight about 1 lb
450 g/1 lb shoulder of venison		1 lb shoulder of venison
1 medium onion, skinned and chopped		1 medium onion, skinned and chopped
450 g/1 lb pork sausagemeat		1 lb bulk sausage
1 garlic clove, skinned and crushed		1 garlic clove, skinned and crushed
5 ml/1 tsp dried marjoram		1 tsp dried marjoram
pinch of ground mace		pinch of ground mace
6 juniper berries, crushed		6 juniper berries, crushed
salt and pepper		salt and pepper
slices of onion and carrot, 6 black peppercorns and 1 bay leaf for flavouring		slices of onion and carrot, 6 black peppercorns and 1 bay leaf for flavoring
1 egg, beaten, to glaze		1 medium egg, beaten, to glaze
5 ml/1 tsp gelatine		1 tsp gelatine
Hot-water pastry		*Hot-water pastry*
350 g/12 oz plain flour		2 cups all-purpose flour
5 ml/1 tsp salt		1 tsp salt
150 g/5 oz lard		$\frac{2}{3}$ cup shortening
150 ml/$\frac{1}{4}$ pint water		$\frac{2}{3}$ cup water

Oven: 425°F/220°C/Mark 7
then 350°F/180°C/Mark 4
Serves 10

Remove the flesh from the pheasant and rabbit joints and cut into small pieces, discarding the skin. Reserve the pheasant carcass and rabbit bones. Cut the venison into similar sized pieces. Place the meats in a bowl with the onion, sausage-meat, garlic, marjoram, spices, juniper and seasonings. Mix thoroughly together, cover and leave in a cool place overnight. Meanwhile, place the pheasant carcass and rabbit bones in a large saucepan with the flavouring ingredients and 1.4 litres/2$\frac{1}{2}$ pints/5 cups water. Bring to the boil, skim, then cover and simmer for 2$\frac{1}{2}$ hours. Strain, then, if necessary, boil to reduce the stock to 300 ml/$\frac{1}{2}$ pint/1$\frac{1}{4}$ cups. Cool, then refrigerate until needed.

The next day, make the pastry. Sift the flour and salt into a bowl and make a well in the centre. Heat the lard and water together, bring to the boil, then pour into the well. Using a wooden spoon, quickly beat the ingredients together, then knead lightly against the side of

the bowl until smooth. Cover with a damp tea towel and leave in a warm place to rest for 40 minutes. Use the pastry while still warm. Keep one quarter of the pastry covered. On a lightly floured surface, roll out the remaining pastry to a 35.5 cm/14 inch round. Fold loosely over the rolling pin, then lift over a 20.5 cm/8 inch spring release tin. Ease the pastry into the corners and press evenly up the sides of the tin. Fold excess pastry outwards over the side of the tin and leave for 1 hour. Spoon the meat mixture into the lined tin, pressing down with the back of the spoon. Roll out the remaining pastry to a 23 cm/9 inch round and use to cover the top of the pie. Seal well, then trim the edges. Flute the edges and make a small hole in the centre of the pie to pour the stock through later. Use the pastry trimmings to make 'leaves' and arrange on top of the pie. Place the pie on a baking sheet and brush with the beaten egg. Bake for 20 minutes, then reduce the temperature and cook for a further 1¾ hours. Take out of the oven, carefully remove the sides of the tin and brush the pastry with beaten egg. Cook for a further 1 hour, covering with foil if the pie becomes too brown. Leave to cool.

Sprinkle the gelatine in 20 ml/4 tsp/4 tsp water in a small bowl and leave to soak for 2–3 minutes. Place the bowl over a saucepan of simmering water and stir until dissolved. Heat the stock in a saucepan and stir in the gelatine. Remove from the heat and leave to cool until just beginning to set. Place the pie on a plate. Pour the stock into the pie through the hole in the top. Cover loosely, then refrigerate overnight or until the jelly has set. Serve cold, cut into thick slices.

HOLY INNOCENTS SAUCE

'Not cold turkey again,' goes up the cry, when the *formerly* festive bird appears on the table for the fourth consecutive day—Holy Innocents Day. A deliciously fresh-flavoured, slightly piquant herb sauce to titillate jaded palates and considerably rejuvenate the slightly tired turkey.

METRIC/IMPERIAL	CUP MEASURES
½ bunch watercress	½ bunch watercress
1 clove garlic, crushed	1 clove garlic, crushed
15 ml/1 tbsp chopped parsley	1 tbsp chopped parsley
15 ml/1 tbsp chopped chives	1 tbsp chopped chives
15 ml/1 tbsp chopped tarragon	1 tbsp chopped tarragon
15 ml/1 tbsp chopped chervil	1 tbsp chopped chervil
5 ml/1 tsp anchovy purée	1 tsp anchovy purée
30 ml/2 tbsp wine vinegar	2 tbsp wine vinegar
2.5 ml/½ tsp French mustard	½ tsp mustard
150 ml/¼ pint virgin olive oil	⅔ cup virgin olive oil
freshly milled black pepper	freshly milled black pepper
salt, to taste	salt, to taste

Serves 6–8

Chop off 2.5 cm/1 inch of the watercress stalks. Put into a blender or food processor with all the remaining ingredients and whizz until they form a smooth purée. Taste, and add a little salt if necessary, but the anchovy purée may be sufficient.

Christmas Dinners

'After a good meal you can forgive anyone, even your own family,' declared Oscar Wilde with his customary perception, and Christmas dinner is the one occasion during the year when even warring families become harmonious. Mercifully, it also remains the one day in which fast food is anathema and people dine leisurely in the manner of their grandparents and great-grandparents, with—one hopes—as much happiness as the Cratchit family in Charles Dickens's *A Christmas Carol*:

'Such a bustle ensued that you might have thought a goose the rarest of all birds; a feathered phenomenon, to which a black swan was a matter of course.... Mrs Cratchit made the gravy (ready beforehand in a little saucepan) hissing hot; Master Peter mashed the potatoes with incredible vigour; Miss Belinda sweetened up the apple-sauce; Martha dusted the hot plates .... At last the dishes were set on, and grace was said. It was succeeded by a breathless pause, as Mrs Cratchit, looking slowly all along the carving-knife, prepared to plunge it in the breast; but when she did, and when the long expected gush of stuffing issued forth, one murmer of delight arose all round the board ....
'There never was such a goose .... Its tenderness and flavour ...'.

In Dickens's time turkey was a greater luxury than goose, and on Christmas morning when the penitent Scrooge woke from his dream he sent a boy to the poulterer to buy the Cratchits the prize turkey . . . '"Not the little prize turkey, the big one." "What! The one as big as me?" returned the boy'.

By the time Alison Uttley wrote *The Country Child* in 1930, however, turkey had become well established as the classic fare:

'The turkey was not basted, and the bread-sauce forgotten, but everyone worked with a will and soon all was ready and piping hot.

'The potatoes were balls of snow, the sprouts green as if they had just come from the garden, as indeed they had, for they too had been dug out of the snow not long before. The turkey was brown and crisp . . . the stuffing smelled of summer and the herb garden in the heat of the sun.'

Christmas Crackers

Crackers are now as indispensable to Christmas dinner as mince pies and pudding, but they have only been with us for just over 100 years, and were the brainchild of a Victorian pâtissier and confectioner named Thomas Smith.

On a holiday in France he had seen, for the first time, sugared almonds, wrapped in coloured paper with a twist at both ends. Thinking them delightful and unusual, he had brought the idea back to England where, for a time, their novelty made them successful, but after a while sales dwindled. To revitalize them he had tried putting a little motto in each one, which improved the situation a little, but not enough. Somewha despondent, one Christmas he was staring int the open hearth, when suddenly one of the log gave a large crackle.

He was, literally, fired with enthusiasm. only he could make a safe, gentle explosion fo his wrapped *bonbon*, it was possible they coul be as profitable as he had originally dreamed After considerable experimenting he manage to make the bang by the friction of two chem cally impregnated strips of cardboard bein pulled. He then went on to make what is no the traditional cracker, inserting almonds an mottoes.

Crackers or 'cosaques', as they were als known, became one of the great success storie of the century. Gradually the sugared almond were replaced with trinkets and paper hats, an the designs became more ornate. Inevitably number of other firms joined the cracker band wagon, but Thomas Smith felt that his cracker were unquestionably superior, as his advertise ments show: 'Thomas Smith and Compan have endeavoured by employing special artist to produce designs, the finest modern applianc to interpret their work, and combine Art wit Amusement and Fun with Refinement, to rais the degenerate cosaque from its low state gaudiness and vulgarity to one of elegance an good taste . . . the Mottoes, instead of the usu doggerel, are graceful and epigrammatic, havir been specially written for Tom Smith's Cracke by well-known Authors.'

Such was the success of the firm of Thom Smith that by 1898 they were making 13 millio crackers a year and exporting them to ever corner of the British Empire.

$\mathcal{R}$oast Turkey

According to a seventeenth-century school jingle,

> 'Turkeys, heresy, hops and beer
> Came into England, all in one year.'

Historians vary in their opinion as to when, between 1523 and 1542, turkeys actually arrived in Britain from America; certainly, during this period, the dissolution of the monasteries was in full swing and the people of the south of England had started showing a marked preference for Flemish-style, hop-flavoured beer, to old English ale.

Towards the end of the sixteenth century, turkeys started to replace exotic birds such as swans, peacocks and bustards as Christmas fare in many of the great houses. James I is reputed to be the person who first made turkey popular in England as he abhorred any form of pork, and turkey therefore replaced pork at a number of banquets and ceremonial occasions. However, it was several centuries before turkey became the Christmas staple as it is today. The Victorians and Edwardians loved their food to look elaborate and would often decorate the Christmas bird with coloured paper streamers. Another popular practice was to keep the accompanying sausages in links and festoon them round the bird, like an alderman's chains.

Turkey can be dry, so it is important to baste well during cooking. No Christmas bird is complete without its stuffings, and these also help to keep the bird moist, as well as adding flavour—and one must not forget the final garnish of sausages and bacon rolls.

ROAST TURKEY WITH CHESTNUT AND SAUSAGEMEAT STUFFING

METRIC/IMPERIAL	CUP MEASURES
5.5 kg/12 lb oven-ready turkey	12 lb oven-ready turkey
chestnut stuffing (see overleaf)	chestnut stuffing (see overleaf)
sausagemeat stuffing (see overleaf)	sausagemeat stuffing (see overleaf)
50 g/2 oz butter	4 tbsp/½ stick butter
salt and freshly milled black pepper	salt and freshly milled black pepper
6 rashers streaky bacon	6 streaky bacon slices

Oven: 350°F/180°C/Mark 4
Serves 8–12

Wipe the bird inside and out with a clean, damp cloth. Stuff the neck end with chestnut stuffing.

Stuff the main cavity with the sausagemeat stuffing or, alternatively put the stuffing into an oven-proof dish and cook for 1 hour.

Put into a meat tin and spread with the butter. Season with salt and pepper. Lay the bacon over the breast and cover the whole tin loosely with

CHESTNUT STUFFING

METRIC/IMPERIAL	•	CUP MEASURES
450 g/1 lb chestnuts		1 lb chestnuts
150 ml/¼ pint turkey stock		⅔ cup turkey stock
75 g/3 oz fresh white breadcrumbs		1½ cups fresh white breadcrumbs
grated rind of 1 small orange		grated rind of 1 small orange
1 egg, beaten		1 medium egg, beaten
salt and freshly milled black pepper		salt and freshly milled black pepper

foil. Roast for 4 hours, basting frequently, and remove the foil for the last 40 minutes cooking.
Make a small slit in the top of each chestnut. Put into boiling water for 5 minutes, then peel off the shells. Keep the chestnuts in the water while preparing them and if, halfway through, they start becoming difficult to peel, replace the saucepan over the heat and bring back to the boil. Put into a clean saucepan with the turkey stock, cover and simmer gently for about 20 minutes or until the chestnuts are tender. Purée the chestnuts together with the stock in a blender or food processor, then tip into a mixing bowl. Stir in the breadcrumbs, then the orange rind and finally the beaten egg. Season with salt and freshly milled black pepper.

SAUSAGEMEAT STUFFING

METRIC/IMPERIAL	•	CUP MEASURES
the turkey heart and liver		the turkey heart and liver
25 g/1 oz butter		2 tbsp butter
450 g/1 lb pork sausagemeat		1 lb bulk sausage
1 medium onion, finely chopped		1 medium onion, finely chopped
1 stick celery, finely chopped		1 stick celery, finely chopped
30 ml/2 tbsp chopped parsley		2 tbsp chopped parsley
15 ml/1 tbsp chopped thyme		1 tbsp chopped thyme
225 g/8 oz fresh white breadcrumbs		4 cups fresh white breadcrumbs
5 ml/1 tsp salt		1 tsp salt
1.25 ml/¼ tsp freshly milled black pepper		¼ tsp freshly milled black pepper
grated rind and juice of 1 lemon		grated rind and juice of 1 lemon
2 eggs, beaten		2 medium eggs, beaten

Chop the turkey heart and liver finely and fry in the butter for 5 minutes. Add all the remaining ingredients and mix well.

CRANBERRY SAUCE

No New England Thanksgiving Dinner would be complete without cranberry sauce to serve with the turkey, but since the end of the last war it has gradually become an accepted part of Christmas dinner. Its sharp flavour combines well with both turkey and ham, and it is as good with cold meats as with hot.

Almost all the fresh cranberries available in

'At Ambergate my sister had sent a motor car for us—so we were at Ripley in time for turkey and Christmas pudding. My God, what masses of food here, turkey, large tongues, long wall of roast loin of pork, pork-pies, sausages, mince pies, dark cakes covered with almonds, cheese-cakes, lemon-tarts, jellies, endless masses of food with whisky, gin, port wine, burgundy, muscatel. It seems incredible. We played charades—the old people of 67 playing away harder than the young ones—and lit the Christmas tree, and drank healths, and sang and roared—Lord above.'

Selected Letters, D. H. Lawrence

e UK come from across the Atlantic but a ightly smaller variety is found in northern urope.

—METRIC/IMPERIAL—	• ——CUP MEASURES——
50 g/12 oz cranberries, washed	3 cups cranberries, washed
350 g/12 oz sugar	1½ cups sugar
30 ml/2 tbsp port	2 tbsp port

Serves 8 10

ut the cranberries in a saucepan, cover with 00 ml/½ pint/1¼ cups cold water and bring slowly) the boil over a moderate heat. Simmer,

uncovered, for a further 10 minutes or until the berries have burst. Add the sugar and port and cook very gently until the sugar has dissolved. Cool before serving.

BREAD SAUCE

The traditional accompaniment to chicken, turkey and game such as pheasant and grouse, bread sauce is Scots in origin. A good bread sauce should not be a bland affair but well-flavoured with cloves, nutmeg or mace, and plenty of freshly milled black pepper.

METRIC/IMPERIAL	CUP MEASURES
2 cloves	2 cloves
1 medium onion, skinned	1 medium onion, skinned
1 blade of mace or a small piece of nutmeg	1 blade of mace or a small piece of nutmeg
450 ml/¾ pint milk	2 cups milk
75 g/3 oz fresh white breadcrumbs	1½ cups fresh white breadcrumbs
salt and pepper	salt and pepper
15 g/½ oz butter	1 tbsp butter
30 ml/2 tbsp single cream	2 tbsp light cream

Serves 6

Stick the cloves into the onion and place in a small heavy-based pan with the mace or nutmeg and milk. Bring slowly to the boil, remove from the heat, cover and leave to infuse for 10 minutes. Remove the onion and mace or nutmeg, then add the breadcrumbs and salt and pepper to taste. Return to the heat and simmer gently for 10–15 minutes, stirring occasionally. Stir in the butter and cream.

Plum Pudding

Originally a medieval porridge or pottage mad with meat broth, raisins, prunes, spices, fru juice and wine thickened with brown brea crumbs, plum pudding used to be served at th *beginning* of a meal. By the end of the seve teenth century it started to become a stiff mixture and finally in the eighteenth century became a round ball of pudding, boiled in cloth.

By tradition, the plum pudding for Chris mas should be stirred by all the family to brin them luck and should be made on the Sunda before Advent, known as 'Stir-Up Sunday This did not originally refer to the pudding, bu to the Collect for the 25th Sunday after Trini which reads, 'Stir up, we beseech thee, O Lor the wills of thy fruitful people; that the plenteously bringing forth the fruit of goo works, may be of thee plenteously rewarde This was altered down the ages by cheeky cho boys to:

> 'Stir up, we beseech thee,
> The pudding in the pot
> And when we get home
> We'll eat it all hot!'

The silver coins and trinkets in the puddin used to be more symbolic than they are toda Only one silver coin was added, promisin wealth to the person whose portion it was in. silver ring prophesied a speedy marriage, whi a thimble foresaw the worst possible end for young girl—the life of an old maid!

OLD-FASHIONED PLUM PUDDING

METRIC/IMPERIAL	CUP MEASURES
100 g/4 oz prunes, stoned and chopped	½ cup prunes, stoned and chopped
175 g/6 oz currants	1 cup currants
175 g/6 oz seedless raisins	1 cup seedless raisins
175 g/6 oz sultanas	1 cup sultanas
25 g/1 oz blanched almonds, chopped	2 tbsp blanched almonds, chopped
finely grated rind and juice of 1 lemon	finely grated rind and juice of 1 lemon
100 g/4 oz plain flour	¾ cup all-purpose flour
2.5 ml/½ tsp grated nutmeg	½ tsp grated nutmeg
2.5 ml/½ tsp ground cinnamon	½ tsp ground cinnamon
2.5 ml/½ tsp salt	½ tsp salt
75 g/3 oz fresh breadcrumbs	1½ cups fresh breadcrumbs
00 g/4 oz shredded suet	1 cup shredded suet
100 g/4 oz soft dark brown sugar	½ cup soft dark brown sugar
2 eggs, beaten	2 medium eggs, beaten
150 ml/¼ pint brown ale	⅔ cup brown ale
150 ml/¼ pint brandy, rum or sherry	⅔ cup brandy, rum or sherry
holly sprig, to decorate	holly sprig, to decorate
75 ml/5 tbsp brandy, to flame	5 tbsp brandy, to flame
brandy or rum butter (page 33) or cream, to serve	brandy or rum butter (page 33) or light or heavy cream, to serve

Serves 8

Place the dried fruits in a large bowl with the nuts, lemon rind and juice. Mix well. In a separate bowl, sift together the flour, nutmeg, cinnamon and salt. Add the breadcrumbs, suet and sugar and mix. Pour in the beaten egg and brown ale, beat well, then stir in the dried fruit mixture until evenly incorporated. Cover the bowl with cling film and leave to stand in a cool place for 24 hours.

The next day, add the brandy, rum or sherry, stirring well. Butter a 1.7 litre/3 pint/7½ cup pudding basin and pack in the pudding mixture, pushing it down well. Cover the basin with pleated greaseproof paper and foil and secure tightly with string. Place in a large saucepan filled with enough boiling water to come half-way up the sides of the basin. Bring to the boil and steam the pudding for 4−5 hours, topping up with boiling water when necessary. Remove the pudding from the pan and allow to cool completely for 1−2 hours. Uncover the pudding, then re-cover with fresh greaseproof paper and foil. Store in a cool, dry place for at least 1 month (or up to 1 year).

To serve, steam in the same way for 2−3 hours. Turn out on to a warmed serving dish and put a sprig of holly in the middle.

To flame the pudding, warm the brandy gently in a small saucepan, pour over the pudding and light carefully with a match.

MINCE PIES

The original mince pies were baked in the shape of a crib and were exchanged between families on Christmas Eve. Being given a mince pie baked by another cook was supposed to bring good luck for one calendar month for the household, so it was considered prudent to make quite certain you received (and gave in return)

Now thrice welcome, Christmas,
Which brings us good cheer,
Minc'd pies and plum porridge,
Good ale and strong beer;
With pig, goose and capon,
The best that can be,
So well doth the weather
and our stomachs agree

Anon

twelve pies to ensure prosperity and happiness for the forthcoming year.

A pretty idea for Christmas is to decorate the top of the pies with festive shapes. Roll out the pastry trimmings and cut out holly leaves, then roll little balls of pastry to make berries. Stick the shapes on top of the pies with water, then paint the leaves green with edible food colouring, and the berries red.

If kept in an airtight tin, mince pies will keep for about a month.

METRIC/IMPERIAL	•	CUP MEASURES
350 g/12 oz plain flour		2 cups all-purpose flour
175 g/6 oz butter		$\frac{3}{4}$ cup butter
700 g/1½ lb mincemeat (see page 61)		2 cups mincemeat (see page 61)
1 egg white		1 large egg white
caster sugar		superfine sugar
cream or brandy butter (see right), to serve		cream or brandy butter (see right), to serve

Oven: 400°F/200°C/Mark 6
Makes 12 large pies

ft the flour into a bowl, then rub in the butter ntil the mixture resembles fine breadcrumbs. ind to a firm dough with about 60 ml/4 tbsp/ tbsp water. Knead lightly until just smooth. 'rap and chill in the refrigerator for 20 minutes.

Roll out the pastry thinly on a floured surface d cut out twenty-four 10 cm/4 inch rounds, -rolling as necessary. Place half the rounds on aking sheets and spoon mincemeat on to the entre of each. Brush the pastry edges with ater. Cover with the remaining pastry rounds, aling the edges well. Knock up the pastry lges and flute them if wished. Bake for 15 inutes.

Remove the pies from the oven, brush with ghtly beaten egg white and dredge with caster r superfine sugar. Return to the oven for a rther 5–7 minutes.

Serve the mince pies hot or warm, with cream r brandy butter in a separate bowl. (Pies will st over the Christmas period—just pop them a hot oven to rejuvenate.)

ℬrandy and Rum Butters

randy is the spirit most commonly used these ays, but it was rum which was used in the riginal 'hard sauce'. Cumberland Rum Butter pread on warm oatcakes or scones was always erved to welcome a new baby and at Christen- gs in the north-west of England. The butter as supposed to promise the goodness of life, um—the spirit of life, sugar—the sweetness of fe, and nutmeg (an essential ingredient of rum, ut not brandy, butter)—the spice of life.

Whether it was its connection with new-born babies that caused it gradually to become accepted throughout the British Isles as the perfect accompaniment to plum pudding and mince pies, or simply because the combination tasted good, history does not relate, but it is now rarely eaten at any other time of year. Pots of Cumberland Rum Butter, however, can be found in most high-class delicatessens and food halls throughout the year.

BRANDY BUTTER

——METRIC/IMPERIAL——	——CUP MEASURES——
100 g/4 oz butter, softened	8 tbsp /1 stick butter, softened
100 g/4 oz icing sugar, sifted	1 cup confectioners' sugar, sifted
45 ml/3 tbsp brandy	3 tbsp brandy

Serves 8

Beat the butter in a bowl until pale and light. Gradually beat in the icing or confectioners' sugar, alternately with the brandy. Beat until light and fluffy. Pile into a small dish and leave to harden before serving.

RUM BUTTER

Follow the recipe for Brandy Butter, but use soft brown sugar instead of the icing or confectioners' sugar, and replace the brandy by 45 ml/3 tbsp/3 tbsp rum and add a pinch of grated nutmeg.

The Food of Old England

Christmas food is customarily plenteous. In 1289 the Bishop of Hereford's 41 guests (plus their attendant servants) managed to consume in one day, among other things, two calves, four does, four pigs, 60 fowl, 18 partridges, two geese, and cheese and bread in 'proportion', as well as an 'unscored amount of beer, 40 gallons of red wine and four of white'. In 1399 Richard II gave a series of feasts in the Great Hall at Westminster, 'and such numbers came that every day there were slain, 26 or 28 oxen and 300 sheep, besides fowls without number.' Even allowing for the fact that their animals were not as muscular as today's, and for apparently gargantuan appetites this quantity of food must have fed a prodigious number. It is also recorded that in 1507 Edward Stafford, Duke of Buckingham, gave a vast banquet for no fewer than 459 people at Thornbury Castle on Twelfth Night.

That great chronicler Samuel Pepys, does not appear to have fared so well in 1662, but whether that was because his wife had been ill, or because it was so soon after the restoration of the monarchy, he does not recount. For, after attending church, he 'walked home again with great pleasure having there dined by my wife' edside with great content, having a mess of brave plum-porridge, and a roast pullet for dinner and I sent for a mince pie abroad, my wife not being well enough to make any herself yet.'

The special Christmas menu and the desire to eat well amazed Victoire de Soligny, the chronicler, who wrote in 1823, 'This English custom of having a particular fare for this particular day is perhaps without exception the most universal of any that prevails in this country. Probably there is not a single table spread on Christmas Day throughout the land—from the King's to the lowest artizan's that can scrape together enough to buy him dinner at all—that is not furnished with roast beef and plum pudding.'

*R*oast Goose

For centuries goose was the festive fowl, served on Christmas Day and Michaelmas Day (29th September). Some people felt that Michaelmas geese, which were younger and reared on summer grass and gleanings from the stubble fields after the harvest, were superior to the older, fatter Christmas geese. To counteract any greasiness, the Christmas goose, unlike its Michaelmas brother which was often simply roasted, was always stuffed, either with sage and onion, or fruit such as apple, quince, pear or prune.

When buying a bird, bear in mind that goose melts like a candle and huge birds virtually vanish before your eyes. To make certain a goose is cooked to perfection and not greasy there are two golden rules. Firstly, before roast-

ing, the skin must be pricked all over with a fork, and this should be repeated two or three times during cooking. This ensures that as much fat as possible comes out of the bird. Secondly, the bird must be stood on a trivet so that the fat can drip into the roasting tin beneath; if necessary empty the tin a couple of times during cooking (but *don't throw the fat away*— see Goose Grease). Stick to the rules and the skin will be crisp and brown, the flesh moist, and you will have a feast fit for a king.

ROAST GOOSE WITH PRUNE STUFFING

METRIC/IMPERIAL	CUP MEASURES
4–5 kg/9–11 lb oven-ready goose (with giblets)	9–11 lb oven-ready goose (with giblets)
salt and freshly ground pepper	salt and freshly ground pepper
450 g/1 lb prunes, soaked overnight	2¼ cups prunes, soaked overnight
300 ml/½ pint dry white wine	1¼ cups dry white wine
50 g/2 oz butter	4 tbsp/½ stick butter
1 small onion, skinned and finely chopped	1 small onion, skinned and finely chopped
30 ml/2 tbsp port	2 tbsp port
100 g/4 oz fresh breadcrumbs	2 cups fresh breadcrumbs
5 ml/1 tsp plain flour	1 tsp all-purpose flour

Oven: 400°F/200°C/Mark 6
Serves 8–10

Pull inside fat out of the goose and reserve. Prick the skin of the goose with a fork in several places. Rub salt over the skin. Drain the prunes and place in a saucepan with the wine. Bring to the boil and simmer for about 10 minutes or until tender. Remove the prunes from the cooking liquid, discard the stones, chop the flesh and put in a bowl. Reserve the cooking liquid. Melt $40\,g/1\frac{1}{2}\,oz/3$ tbsp of the butter in another pan, add the onion and cook gently until soft but not coloured. Separate the goose liver from the giblets and chop finely. Add to the onion and cook gently for 2–3 minutes, then mix with the prunes. Deglaze the pan with the port, scraping the pan to dislodge any sediment. Pour the liquid into the prune mixture, add the breadcrumbs and mix well. Allow to cool for 10 minutes.

Spoon the stuffing into the neck cavity of the goose. Skewer the neck skin to the back of the bird, then truss and tie up the goose with string. Weigh the bird and calculate the cooking time allowing 15 minutes per $450\,g/1\,lb$ plus 1

GOOSE GREASE

Always referred to as grease, as it is softer than the fat of other poultry, the grease from the Christmas goose used to be as highly prized as the meat itself. Excellent for general cooking purposes, such as roasting and frying, its richness and flavour improves many dishes and its purity makes it ideal for sealing food, such as potted meats (see page 59). To bread-and-dripping connoisseurs it is the unrivalled king, and it was considered a great delicacy when beaten with vinegar, lemon juice, finely chopped onion and parsley and used as a sandwich filling.

minutes. Put the goose on a wire rack in a roasting tin and put in the oven.

When the goose is cooked, transfer to a serving dish and keep warm in a low oven. Pour off all but 30 ml/2 tbsp/2 tbsp fat from the juices in the roasting tin. Transfer to the top of the cooker and blend in the flour. Cook for 1 minute until just colouring, then slowly add the reserved prune liquid, stirring well. Bring to the boil and simmer for 2–3 minutes. Season to taste and whisk in the remaining butter to give the sauce a good shine. Serve the sauce separately.

ROAST CAPON WITH APRICOT AND WALNUT STUFFING

Presents to the landlord to keep him sweet on quarter-days (when quarterly rents were due) were customary for centuries, and capons (castrated cocks) were the most usual Christmas and New Year offerings. One anonymous writer in 1644 insisted that one should 'offer up a capon sacrifice unto his worship at a New Year's Tide', while another popular rhyme was:

And when the tenants come to pay their quarter's rent,

They bring some fowls at Midsummer, a dish of fish at Lent

At Christmas a capon, at Michaelmas a goose,

And somewhat else at New Year's Tide, for fear their lease fly loose!

Capons vary in size from 2.25 kg/5 lb to 3.5 kg/8 lb and will comfortably serve 8–12 people.

METRIC/IMPERIAL •	CUP MEASURES
1 oven-ready capon	1 oven-ready capon
salt and freshly milled black pepper	salt and freshly milled black pepper
For the Stuffing	*For the Stuffing*
75 g/3 oz butter	6 tbsp butter
2 medium-sized onions, skinned and finely chopped	2 medium-sized onions, skinned and finely chopped
175 g/6 oz fresh white breadcrumbs	3 cups fresh white breadcrumbs
grated rind and juice of 1 orange	grated rind and juice of 1 orange
100 g/4 oz dried apricots, finely chopped	$\frac{5}{8}$ cup dried apricots, finely chopped
50 g/2 oz walnuts, finely chopped	$\frac{1}{2}$ cup walnuts, finely chopped
15 ml/1 tbsp finely chopped fresh rosemary	1 tbsp finely chopped fresh rosemary
salt and freshly milled black pepper	salt and freshly milled black pepper

Oven: 375°F/190°C/Mark 5
Serves 8–12

Remove any large pieces of fat from the bird and put on one side. Melt the butter in a pan and gently fry the onions for 5 minutes. Remove from the heat and tip into a mixing bowl. Add all the remaining stuffing ingredients and mix well. Divide the stuffing between the neck end and the cavity of the bird. Truss with string.

Weigh and calculate the cooking time, allowing 15 minutes per 450 g/1 lb and 15 minutes over, including the weight of the stuffing. Place the bird in a roasting tin, season lightly with salt and pepper and lay the reserved pieces of chicken fat on the breast. Roast until crisp and golden brown, basting frequently during cooking.

COLD SPICED BEEF

Beef featured strongly on Christmas menus right up until the middle of the nineteenth century, but it was the Elizabethans who were particularly fond of this kind of spiced beef. Boiling was the most usual method of cooking, but there are some old recipes in which the meat is very slowly pot-roasted.

METRIC/IMPERIAL •	CUP MEASURES
1.8 kg/4 lb boned brisket of beef	4 lb boned brisket of beef
250 g/10 oz coarse sea salt	1¼ cups coarse sea salt
2 shallots, finely chopped	2 shallots, finely chopped
3 bay leaves	3 bay leaves
5 ml/1 tsp saltpetre	1 tsp saltpetre
5 ml/1 tsp ground allspice	1 tsp ground allspice
90 ml/6 tbsp brown sugar	6 tbsp brown sugar
5 ml/1 tsp ground cloves	1 tsp ground cloves
5 ml/1 tsp ground mace	1 tsp ground mace
6 peppercorns, lightly crushed	6 peppercorns, lightly crushed
15 ml/1 tbsp chopped fresh thyme	1 tbsp chopped fresh thyme
1 onion, skinned and chopped	1 onion, skinned and chopped
2 carrots, peeled and chopped	2 carrots, peeled and chopped

Serves 10

Put the meat into a large bowl. Rub it on all sides with 225 g/8 oz/1 cup of the salt. Cover and leave for 24 hours in a refrigerator or cool place. Add the remaining salt to the bowl with the shallots, bay leaves, saltpetre, allspice, brown sugar, cloves, mace, peppercorns and thyme. Rub this well into the beef and leave for 7 days, turning the beef and rubbing it well with the spice mixture every day. Pour off any liquid which forms.

Remove the meat from the bowl, roll up and tie securely with string. Put the meat into a large saucepan with the onion and carrots. Cover with cold water and bring slowly to simmering point. Remove any scum, then cover and simmer *very gently* for 4–5 hours or until the meat is very tender. Allow to cool in the cooking liquor, then lift it out. Place it between two boards with a heavy weight on top and leave to press overnight.

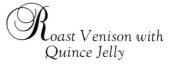

Roast Venison with Quince Jelly

Once described as 'a great meat for great men', available only to the nobility who hunted it, venison (the meat of the deer) can now be enjoyed by all. Quinces were a very popular Tudor fruit, and Henry VIII's passion for hunting deer was legendary, so it was perhaps inevitable they should end up in a dish together.

ROAST VENISON

Venison is inclined to be tough so it is hung for 1–2 weeks before cooking. The meat should be dark and firm with clear white fat. As there is only a little fat on venison, the meat tends to be dry, so additional fat or liquid is added for cooking. For quince jelly, see page 60.

METRIC/IMPERIAL	CUP MEASURES
2 carrots, chopped	2 medium carrots, chopped
1 small onion, chopped	1 small onion, chopped
1 celery stick, chopped	1 celery stick, chopped
6 black peppercorns	6 black peppercorns
parsley stalk	parsley stalk
1 bay leaf	1 bay leaf
3 blades of mace	3 blades of mace
red wine	red wine
saddle, haunch or shoulder of venison	saddle, haunch or shoulder of venison
melted butter or margarine or vegetable oil	melted butter or margarine or vegetable oil
15 ml/1 tbsp flour	1 tbsp all-purpose flour
300 ml/½ pint beef stock	1¼ cups beef stock

Oven: 325°F/170°C/Mark 3

Place the carrot, onion, celery, peppercorn, parsley, bay leaf and blades of mace in a large dish. Add the venison and sufficient wine to half-cover. Leave to marinate for 12 hours, turning the meat 2–3 times. Remove the meat and pat dry with absorbent kitchen paper. Place on a large piece of foil. Brush generously with butter. Fold the foil to make a parcel. Weigh. Place the parcel in a roasting tin and roast in the oven allowing 25 minutes per 450 g/1 lb. Fold back the foil 20 minutes before the end of the cooking time to allow to brown. For gravy, pour off most of the fat from the roasting tin leaving about 30 ml/2 tbsp of the sediment. Stir in about 15 ml/1 level tbsp flour, blend well and cook slowly over the heat until it turns brown, stirring. Slowly stir in the stock and boil for 2–3 minutes. Season well, and strain.

MEDIEVAL BRAWN

Brawn is a traditional English dish of jellied pork, usually flavoured with herbs and spices. 'The shield of brawn' was the *pièce de résistance* at every medieval Christmas banquet. An intricately moulded and castellated creation, decorated with piped cream and even gilded with gold leaf, it would take many hours of concentrated work in the kitchen.

METRIC/IMPERIAL	CUP MEASURES
$\frac{1}{2}$ pig's head	$\frac{1}{2}$ pig's head
2 pig's trotters	2 pig's trotters
$\frac{1}{2}$ nutmeg	$\frac{1}{2}$ nutmeg
20 black peppercorns	20 black peppercorns
10 cloves	10 cloves
3 bay leaves	3 bay leaves
2 blades mace	2 blades mace
15 ml/1 tbsp dried sage	1 tbsp dried sage
1 bunch parsley	1 bunch parsley
5 ml/1 tsp salt	1 tsp salt

Serves 6–8

Remove the brains and the eyeball from head if this has not already been done. W the head thoroughly in cold water. Split trotters in half. Grate the nutmeg. Put all ingredients into a large pan. Cover with c water and bring to the boil. Remove any sc from the surface. Cover the pan and simm very gently for about 4 hours or until the m is very tender.

Allow the meat and liquor to cool for ab an hour, then strain the meat, reserving liquor. Take the meat off the bones, discard all the skin, gristle, excess fat, etc. Chop meat finely and put into a 1.2 litre/2 pint/5 c bowl or mould. While doing this boil 600 r 1 pint/2$\frac{1}{2}$ cups of the stock rapidly until it reduced by half. Taste and add a little extra s as necessary. It is important not to add t much salt at first or on reduction the stock c become over-salted. Strain over the meat, th leave overnight to set in a cool place.

To turn out, quickly dip the basin into a bo of very hot water, then invert on to a serv plate.

SYLLABUB

The word *syllabub* is a corruption of 'Sill', a region of the Champagne country which produced sparkling wine known as Sill or Sille, and 'bub', the common Elizabethan slang for a bubbling drink. The Sill was mixed with frothing cream—thus syllabub.

Elizabethan syllabubs were more liquid than those we enjoy today, and were served at Christmas and other festive occasions in large punch bowls, from which they were drunk, rather than eaten with a spoon.

By the middle of the eighteenth century, it had become more usual to make syllabubs with sherry rather than wine, largely because the Georgians had found that by reducing the amount of wine and sugar the syllabub did not separate so easily.

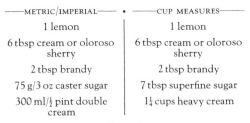

METRIC/IMPERIAL	CUP MEASURES
1 lemon	1 lemon
6 tbsp cream or oloroso sherry	6 tbsp cream or oloroso sherry
2 tbsp brandy	2 tbsp brandy
75 g/3 oz caster sugar	7 tbsp superfine sugar
300 ml/½ pint double cream	1¼ cups heavy cream

Serves 6

Thinly pare the rind from the lemon, put it into a basin and pour over the sherry and brandy. Squeeze the juice from the lemon, add to the bowl, then cover and leave for at least 6 hours or, preferably, overnight.

Strain the liquid into a clean bowl, add the sugar and stir until dissolved. Add the cream, then whisk until the mixture stands in soft peaks. Pile into glasses and chill.

WHAT A BOAR

A boar's head was included in every grand dinner from the time Christmas was first celebrated, and even in 1898 was still one of the centrepieces of Queen Victoria's Table. As early as 1289, it was always presented with a lemon in its mouth, though later, an orange was often used instead.

On the Saturday before Christmas each year, there is a Boar's Head Dinner at Queen's College, Oxford. Said to commemorate a former undergraduate's dramatic escape from a wild boar, by stuffing the copy of Aristotle he had been studying down its throat, the head is ceremoniously carried into the room on a large salver by the head chef. The choir follows singing the famous 'Boar's Head Carol':

Caput aprif defero
(I carry the boar's head)
Redden laudes Domino
(Giving praises to God)

Once the dish has been placed upon the head table, the lemon or orange from the mouth is presented to the chief singer and sprigs of bay and rosemary that garnish it to the guests.

Festive Cakes and Biscuits

Afternoon tea may no longer be the important meal it once was, but Christmas is the one time of year when worries over burgeoning waistlines should be forgotten and the palate titillated with the forbidden temptation of cakes and biscuits.

The rich fruit cake covered with marzipan and royal icing that we now eat on Christmas Day was originally served on Twelfth Night. However, the Twelfth-Night Cake was more elaborately decorated. Instead of simple Father Christmas and reindeer ornaments, or marzipan holly leaves and berries, the Twelfth Night Cake was much larger, resembling a modern wedding cake.

In 1811 a shop in Cheapside advertised a cake which reputedly weighed half a ton and Queen Victoria's cake of 1849 was clearly a splendid affair according to *The Illustrated London News*: 'The cake was of regal dimensions, being about 30 inches in diameter and tall in proportion; round the side the decorations consisted of strips of gilded paper, bowing outwards near the top, issuing from an elegant gold bordering. The figures, of which there were 16, on top of the cake, represented [vignette] of beaux and belles of the last century enjoying a repast *al fresco* under some trees....'

TWELFTH-NIGHT CAKE

──METRIC/IMPERIAL── •	──CUP MEASURES──
350 g/12 oz butter	1½ cups/3 sticks butter
50 g/12 oz caster sugar	1⅔ cups superfine sugar
6 eggs, beaten	6 large eggs, beaten
75 ml/5 tbsp brandy	5 tbsp brandy
350 g/12 oz plain flour	2⅛ cups all-purpose flour
5 ml/1 tsp ground allspice	1 tsp ground allspice
ml/1 tsp ground ginger	1 tsp ground ginger
5 ml/1 tsp ground coriander	1 tsp ground coriander
5 ml/1 tsp ground cinnamon	1 tsp ground cinnamon
00 g/1½ lb mixed dried fruit	4 cups mixed dried fruit
50 g/2 oz blanched almonds, chopped	½ cup blanched almonds, chopped
45 ml/3 tbsp apricot conserve	3 tbsp apricot conserve
900 g/2 lb marzipan	2 lb marzipan
4 egg whites	4 large egg whites
900 g/2 lb icing sugar	8 cups confectioners' sugar
5 ml/1 tbsp lemon juice	1 tbsp lemon juice
10 ml/2 tsp glycerine	2 tsp light corn syrup
lacé fruit, angelica and ilver balls, to decorate	candied fruit, angelica and silver balls, to decorate

Oven: 300°F/150°C/Mark 2
Makes about 30 slices

Grease a deep 25 cm/10 inch round cake tin and line the base and sides with greaseproof paper. Cream the butter and sugar together until pale and fluffy. Gradually add the eggs and then the brandy, beating well after each addition. Fold in the flour, spices, fruits and nuts. Turn into the prepared tin and level the surface. Bake for 2½ hours or until firm to the touch. Cover with paper halfway through cooking if the cake browns too quickly. Leave to cool in the tin for 30 minutes, then turn out and cool completely on a wire rack.

When the cake is cold, wrap in greaseproof paper and either place in a cake tin or wrap in double-thickness foil. Leave to mature for at least 1 month.

To cover with marzipan, heat the apricot conserve in a small saucepan until just melted, then brush over the top and sides of the cake. Measure around the cake with a piece of string. Dust the work surface with icing or confectioners' sugar and roll out two-thirds of the marzipan to a rectangle, half the length of the string by twice the depth of the cake. Trim the edges, then cut in half lengthways with a sharp knife. Gently lift the marzipan and place it firmly in position around the cake. Smooth the joins with a palette knife and keep the top and bottom edges square. Roll a jam jar lightly around the cake to help the paste stick more firmly. Roll out the remaining marzipan to fit the top of the cake. With the help of the rolling pin, lift it on to the cake. Lightly roll with the rolling pin, then smooth the join and leave to dry for up to 4 days before starting to ice.

For the icing, whisk the egg whites until slightly frothy. Then sift and stir in about one quarter of the icing or confectioners' sugar with a wooden spoon. Continue adding more sugar gradually, beating well after each addition, until about three-quarters of the sugar has been added. Beat in the lemon juice and continue beating until the icing is smooth. Beat in the remaining sugar. Finally, stir in the glycerine or light corn syrup to prevent the icing becoming too hard. Cover and keep for 1 day to allow any air bubbles to rise to the surface.

The next day, using two-thirds of the icing, roughly flat-ice the top and sides of the cake. Leave to dry for 24 hours. Spoon the remaining icing on top of the flat icing and roughly smooth over it with a palette knife. Using the palette knife or back of a teaspoon, pull the icing to make rough peaks. Decorate lavishly with the glacé/candied fruit, angelica and silver balls, then leave to dry completely.

STOLLEN

It is on Christmas Eve that *das Christkind*, t Christ child, brings his gifts to German childre before the family sits down to supper. T traditional dish for the evening is carp, a everyone sitting round the table preserves o of the fish's scales to put into their purse, bring them luck and fortune in the coming yea

Stollen, or Christstollen to give it its corre name, comes from Dresden; unlike most yeast breads which stale quickly, the high proportio of fat and fruit means it keeps well, provided is well wrapped.

METRIC/IMPERIAL	•	CUP MEASURES
15 g/½ oz fresh yeast or 7.5 ml/1½ tsp dried yeast plus a pinch of sugar		1½ tsp active dry yeas
100 ml/4 fl oz tepid milk		½ cup tepid milk
225 g/8 oz strong plain flour		1⅜ cups white bread flour
1.25 ml/¼ tsp salt		½ tsp salt
75 g/3 oz butter		6 tbsp butter
grated rind of 1 small lemon		grated rind of 1 smal lemon
50 g/2 oz chopped mixed peel		⅓ cup chopped candie mixed peel
50 g/2 oz currants		⅓ cup currants
50 g/2 oz sultanas		⅓ cup sultanas
25 g/1 oz blanched almonds, chopped		2 tbsp blanched almonds, chopped
½ an egg, beaten		½ a small egg, beaten
icing sugar, to dredge		confectioners' sugar, dredge

Oven: 400°F/200°C/Mark 6
Serves 8–12

rease a large baking sheet. Crumble the fresh
ast into a bowl and cream with the milk until
nooth. If using the dried yeast and sugar,
rinkle the mixture into the milk and leave in a
arm place or 15 minutes until the surface is
othy. Put the flour and salt into a bowl and
b in 50 g/2 oz/4 tbsp of the butter. Add the
mon rind, fruit and nuts. Add the yeast mix-
re and beaten egg and mix to a soft dough.
ırn on to a lightly floured working surface
d knead for about 10 minutes until smooth.
over with a clean cloth and leave to rise in a
arm place for about 1 hour until doubled.
ıead the dough for 2–3 minutes, then roll
to an oval shape about 23 × 18 cm/9 × 7 inches).
ark a line lengthways with the rolling pin.
ırefully fold the dough in half along the marked
ıe. Place on the baking sheet, cover with a
ean cloth and leave in a warm place for about
minutes until doubled in size. Melt the
maining butter and brush over the stollen.
ke in the oven for about 30 minutes until well
sen and golden brown. Transfer to a wire rack
cool. To serve, dredge all over with icing or
nfectioners' sugar.

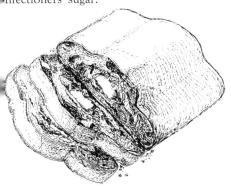

BUCHE DE NOEL

The French have fewer Christmas dishes and
traditions than many of their northern European
neighbours, but the Christmas or Yule Log is
one they share. Most homes boasted a large
open hearth, and on Christmas Eve a large log
usually of oak or ash would be dragged in and
allowed to burn slowly throughout the twelve
days of Christmas. On the day it was brought
in, people paid tribute to it, believing it burnt
away old wrongs and bad luck. A small piece
was always kept which would be carefully pre-
served and stored, ready for lighting the log the
following year.

METRIC/IMPERIAL •	CUP MEASURES
Cake	*Cake*
4 eggs	4 eggs
100 g/4 oz caster sugar	½ cup superfine sugar
75 g/3 oz self-raising flour	½ cup all-purpose flour
	½ tsp baking powder
25 g/1 oz cocoa powder	¼ cup cocoa powder
Filling and Icing	*Filling and Icing*
150 ml/¼ pint milk	⅔ cup milk
2 egg yolks	2 egg yolks
175 g/6 oz plain chocolate, broken into small pieces	6 squares semi-sweet chocolate, broken into small pieces
100 g/4 oz unsalted butter	8 tbsp/1 stick sweet butter
50 g/2 oz icing sugar, sifted	½ cup confectioners' sugar, sifted
extra icing sugar	extra confectioners' sugar
holly to decorate	holly to decorate

Oven: 400°F/200°C/Mark 6
Makes 1 cake

Grease and line a $32.5 \times 22.5\,\text{cm}/13 \times 9$ inch Swiss roll tin (jelly pan). Whisk the eggs and sugar together until thick and creamy, and the whisk leaves a trail when lifted out of the mixture. Sift in the flour and cocoa and fold in. Turn the mixture into the prepared tin. Bake for 12–15 minutes or until the cake springs back when lightly pressed. Turn out on to a piece of greaseproof or non-stick silicone paper dredged with icing or confectioners' sugar. Care-fully peel off the lining paper, trim off the edg and roll up, keeping the paper inside the ro Put to one side and allow to cool.

To make the filling, heat the milk to bloc temperature in a small saucepan. Blend the e yolks in a basin or the top of a double saucepa and beat in the milk. Stand the mixture over pan of gently simmering water and cook, st ring frequently until the mixture coats the ba of a wooden spoon. Add the chocolate and s until it has melted, then remove from the he. Cover the basin or pan with a piece of cling fi and leave to cool, stirring from time to tim Cream the butter and beat in the icing/co fectioners' sugar, then gradually beat in t cooled custard.

Unroll the Swiss roll, and spread with a thi of the filling. Re-roll and spread the outside the roll with the remaining icing. Using a fo mark lines on the top of the log, as if for t bark of a tree. Chill in a refrigerator for abc 1 hour until set, then dust lightly with icing confectioners' sugar and decorate with holly.

Spice Biscuits

Spice biscuits are Christmas fare througho Germany and Scandinavia and often incorp ate as many as seven different spices, rep senting the seven days it took God to create t world.

The crisp, iced German biscuits, or lebkuch were originally baked in monasteries 700 ye ago. Commercially made lebkuchen are bak in special decorative moulds and often ic with intricate patterns.

At Christmas time in Holland, baker's shops and pâtisseries are full of speculaas, some as heavy as 450 g/1 lb, and special moulds (mostly in the shape of men and women) are available for home baking. If you are making them at home, you can use gingerbread men cutters, in which case you will be able to make about 6 men.

SPECULAAS

—METRIC/IMPERIAL— • —CUP MEASURES—	
100 g/4 oz plain white flour	¾ cup all-purpose flour
2.5 ml/½ tsp each of ground cloves, cinnamon and ginger	½ tsp each of ground cloves, cinnamon and ginger
pinch of grated nutmeg	pinch of grated nutmeg
pinch of baking powder	pinch of baking powder
pinch of salt	pinch of salt
50 g/2 oz soft dark brown sugar	¼ cup soft dark brown sugar
15 ml/1 tbsp milk	1 tbsp milk
65 g/2½ oz butter	¼ cup + 1 tbsp butter
30 ml/2 tbsp very finely chopped candied peel	2 tbsp very finely chopped candied peel
flaked blanched almonds, to decorate	flaked blanched almonds, to decorate

Oven: 350°F/180°C/Mark 4
Makes 18

Sift the flour, spices, baking powder and salt into a bowl. Put the sugar and milk in a small saucepan and heat gently, stirring, until the sugar has dissolved. Stir the sugar mixture into the bowl. Add the butter in pieces and the candied peel and work to a smooth dough. Turn the dough onto a floured surface and

knead lightly until no longer sticky. Roll out the dough to a thickness of 0.5 cm/¼ inch. Cut the dough into 18 shapes using a 6.5 cm/2½ inch biscuit cutter and place on greased baking sheets. Press a few almond pieces into each biscuit, then bake in the oven for 15 minutes. Leave to settle on the sheets for a few minutes, then transfer to a wire rack and leave to cool completely. Store in an airtight tin for up to 2 weeks.

PANTOMIMES AT THE RITZ

Tea at the Ritz after the Christmas pantomime is an annual institution. The children sit demurely in their best clothes in the Palm Court while the waiters bring tea, sandwiches and scones. By the time the pretty French cakes and pastries arrive, the little party has become more relaxed and there is the tinkling of laughter as they recall the antics of the pantomime dame or mimic the principal boy.

The pantomime was a Victorian invention whose roots are to be found in the eighteenth-century harlequinade—a comic sketch, often mimed, to entertain the audience between the acts of a play. At first they were simple but clever burlesques, but as their popularity increased they became increasingly lengthy, more sophisticated and bawdy. Victorian sensibilities could not allow the latter, and the escapades of the harlequin gradually gave way to jolly, harmless fairy tales such as Cinderella and Aladdin, with only a touch of rakish humour—totally suitable for children.

LEBKUCHEN

METRIC/IMPERIAL	CUP MEASURES
175 g/6 oz clear honey	$\frac{1}{2}$ cup light honey
50 g/2 oz sugar	$\frac{1}{4}$ cup sugar
30 ml/2 tbsp vegetable oil	2 tbsp vegetable oil
30 ml/2 tbsp water	2 tbsp water
1 egg yolk	1 medium egg yolk
5 ml/1 tsp cocoa powder	1 tsp unsweetened coco
6 drops of lemon oil	6 drops of lemon oil
2.5 ml/$\frac{1}{2}$ tsp ground cardamom	$\frac{1}{2}$ tsp ground cardamor
2.5 ml/$\frac{1}{2}$ tsp ground cinnamon	$\frac{1}{2}$ tsp ground cinnamor
1.25 ml/$\frac{1}{4}$ tsp ground cloves	$\frac{1}{4}$ tsp ground cloves
good pinch of cayenne pepper	good pinch of cayenne pepper
250 g/8 oz flour	$1\frac{3}{8}$ cup all-purpose flou
15 ml/3 tsp baking powder	3 tsp baking powder
75 g/3 oz ground almonds	$\frac{7}{8}$ cup ground almond
75 g/3 oz ground hazelnuts	$\frac{7}{8}$ cup ground hazelnut
75 g/3 oz dried apricots, finely chopped	$\frac{1}{2}$ cup dried apricots, finely chopped
50 g/2 oz mixed peel	$\frac{1}{3}$ cup candied mixed peel
175 g/6 oz icing sugar	$1\frac{1}{2}$ cups confectioners sugar
1 egg white	1 medium egg white

Oven: 325°F/170°C/Mark 3
Makes about 40

Put the honey, sugar, vegetable oil and water a heavy saucepan and heat gently until melte Leave until cold, then stir in the egg yolk, coc powder, lemon oil and spices. Sift the flou

dd two-thirds of the flour to the spice mixture
nd stir well to mix. Mix the remaining flour
ith the nuts, apricots and peel. Add to the
pice mixture and mix well until combined.
urn the dough out onto a floured surface and
nead lightly until it comes together. Roll out
ntil very thin (about 5 mm/¼ inch thick). Stamp
to about 40 shapes using fancy biscuit cutters.
e-roll any odd bits of pastry, if necessary.
tamp out a small hole in some of the biscuits
ith an apple corer, drinking straw or skewer.
eave rest of biscuits plain. Place the biscuit

shapes on greased baking sheets and bake in
batches in the oven for 12–15 minutes until just
beginning to colour. Transfer to a wire rack
until cold and crisp.

Make the icing. Sift the icing or confectioners'
sugar into a bowl, then beat in the egg white and
1–2 drops of warm water to make a thick
spreading consistency. Spread or pipe the icing
immediately over the biscuits and leave on the
wire rack to set for 2–3 hours. Thread coloured
ribbon through the holes in the biscuits and tie
to secure.

LIVERPOOL CHRISTMAS LOAF

When times have been hard at Christmas, wives and mothers have always done everything in their power to give their family as festive a time as possible. During the depression in the 1920s and '30s, northerners devised this yeasted loaf as a replacement for the more expensive Christmas cake. It would be baked in the middle of December and after a week some ale would be poured over it to improve the texture and flavour.

——METRIC/IMPERIAL—— • ——CUP MEASURES——	
Yeast Liquid	*Yeast Liquid*
5 ml/1 tsp sugar	1 tsp sugar
60 ml/4 tbsp warm milk	4 tbsp warm milk
1 egg, beaten	1 medium egg, beaten
15 ml/1 tbsp dried yeast	1 tbsp dry active yeast
Bread	*Bread*
275 g/10 oz strong plain flour	1¾ cups white bread flour
5 ml/1 tsp salt	1 tsp salt
10 ml/2 tsp baking powder	2 tsp baking powder
5 ml/1 tsp grated nutmeg	1 tsp grated nutmeg
10 ml/2 tsp ground mixed spice	2 tsp ground mixed spice
100 g/4 oz lard	½ cup/1 stick shortening
175 g/6 oz soft brown sugar	1 cup soft brown sugar
15 ml/1 tbsp black treacle	1 tbsp molasses
1 egg, beaten	1 medium egg, beaten
350 g/12 oz mixed dried fruit	2 cups mixed dried fruit

Oven: 350°F/180°C/Mark 4
Makes 1 loaf

Grease and flour a 900 g/2 lb/7½ cup loaf tin. Dissolve the sugar in the warm milk, add the beaten egg and mix well. Sprinkle over the dried yeast and leave in a warm place for about 1 minutes or until frothy.

Sift together the flour, salt, baking powder, nutmeg and mixed spice. Cream the lard, sugar and treacle until fluffy, then gradually beat in the egg, a tablespoon at a time. Roughly stir in the flour, then add the fruit and yeast liquid and beat well.

Turn into the prepared tin. Cover with an oiled polythene bag and leave for about 1 hour or until the dough has risen to the top of the tin. Bake for 1 hour. Remove from the oven, turn out of the tin onto a wire rack and leave until cold, then wrap in foil.

50

Yuletide Cocktails

*D*rinking has always played as great a part in Christmas festivities as eating. All the early rhymes and poems urged people to 'make good cheer' and, by all accounts, most of them did just that. It was a time of merry-making, not only for the rich, but also for the poor; for this was the one occasion during the year when masters, mistresses and landlords might be expected to be beneficent. It was inevitable of course that some over-stepped the mark. Jonathan Swift complained in his diary on Christmas Eve, 1711, that he had given Patrick half a crown for his xmas-box, on condition he would be good; and he came home drunk at midnight,' but such behaviour was half-expected.

From the Middle Ages onwards the twelve-day Christmas period was the time for wassailing. Carrying a large bowl, usually made of ash or maple and decorated with ribbons, the poorer people of a parish would tour round, knocking on the doors of the wealthier homes. To the shout of 'wassail'—from the Anglo Saxon *waes heil* meaning 'be whole' or 'be healthy'—they demanded their bowls be filled. Common rewards for their efforts included mulled ale or Lamb's Wool, which were then drunk from the communal bowl. If they were really in luck, they would also be given some food, and occasionally, even money.

In the fruit-growing counties of southern and western England, there was also the tradition of 'wassailing the apple tree'. On Christmas Eve, New Year's Eve or Twelfth Night a party would go out to the orchard carrying a wassail bowl filled with cider. One of the trees would be toasted, then everyone would take a swig from the communal bowl and pour the remainder over the tree's roots to ensure a bounteous harvest for the orchard in the coming year. For many it was just a good excuse for a party, as they would then return to the village for a somewhat rowdy night of revelry.

Wassailing ditties such as these abound. The tunefulness of the song doubtless decreasing in direct proportion to the number of times the bowl was filled!

> *Here we come a-wassailing*
> *Among the leaves so green*
> *Here we come a-wassailing*
> *So fair to be seen*
>
> Anon, Yorkshire
>
> *Good master and mistress, here's a health to*
>   *you we give*
> *And sing jolly wassail as long as we live*
> *And if we do live, 'til another New Year,*
> *Then perhaps we may call, and see who do*
>   *live here*
>
> Anon, West Country

Cocktails

Christmas cocktails should be an extravaganza and these three are old favourites at The Ritz.

CHRISTMAS CAROL

A dreamy concoction of Grand Marnier and Fraise de Bordeaux, with a Scroogist measure of orange juice topped up with champagne.

A Dickens of a good drink.

1 part Grand Marnier	2 parts orange juice
1 part Fraise de Bordeaux	6 parts Ritz champagne

Pour into flute. Decorate with strawberry.

LOG FIRE

...grate amount of Bacardi Gold, kindled with a ...ow of advocaat and enflamed with sambuca ...d a spark of soda water, to give you a hearth-...arming effect.

3 parts Bacardi	dash sambuca
4 parts advocaat	3 parts soda

...nake all ingredients except soda. Pour into ice-...led 'old-fashioned' glass and top up with soda. ...ecorate with red cherry.

CHRISTMAS GLOW

...shining amount of cognac beamed together ...ith Tia Maria and a light measure of ginger ...ine.

2 parts cognac	4 parts ginger wine
4 parts Tia Maria	

...ir ingredients together and strain into a chilled ...ass. Decorate with orange peel.

THE BISHOP

Fine orange well roasted, with wine in a
   cup,
They'll make a sweet bishop when
   gentlefolks sup

                                   Jonathan Swift

...he Bishop is always associated with Oxford ...d Cambridge undergraduates who would brew ...p this drink of port with an orange stuck with ...oves in their rooms. Recipes vary slightly but ...e port, orange and cloves remain constant.

METRIC/IMPERIAL • CUP MEASURES	
8 cloves	8 cloves
2 small oranges	2 small oranges
1 cinnamon stick	1 cinnamon stick
2 pieces blade mace	2 pieces blades of mace
8 allspice berries	8 allspice berries
5 cm/1 inch piece of root ginger, peeled	1 inch piece of root ginger, peeled
grated rind of 1 lemon	grated rind of 1 lemon
4 sugar lumps	4 pieces of lump sugar
1 bottle of port	1 bottle of port
pinch of freshly grated nutmeg	pinch of freshly grated nutmeg

Oven: 325°F/170°C/Mark 3
Serves 6–8

Stick the cloves into the oranges then put in a roasting tin. Bake in the oven for 45 minutes.

Put the cinnamon, mace, allspice and ginger in a saucepan with 300 ml/½ pint/1¼ cups water. Bring to the boil then boil rapidly until reduced by about a third. Put the roasted oranges, sugar and lemon rind in a large warmed serving bowl then pour over the water and spices. Pour the port into a saucepan and heat gently. Do not boil. Pour into the bowl and stir well. Sprinkle with a little grated nutmeg and serve hot.

DR JOHNSON'S PUNCH

'Some people have a foolish way of not minding, or of pretending not to mind, what they eat. For my part I mind my belly very studiously and carefully, for I look upon it that he who does not mind his belly will hardly mind anything else.'

Presumably Dr Johnson also took as much care over what he drank as what he ate, considering it ended up in the same place, and so devised this delicious warm punch to ward off the cold on a winter's day.

——METRIC/IMPERIAL—— •	——CUP MEASURES——
1 orange	1 orange
1 bottle red wine	1 bottle red wine
60 ml/4 tbsp granulated sugar	4 tbsp sugar
3 cloves	3 cloves
3 whole allspice berries	3 whole allspice berries
12.5 cm/$\frac{1}{2}$ inch piece of green ginger, peeled	$\frac{1}{2}$ inch piece of green ginger, peeled
600 ml/1 pint water	2$\frac{1}{2}$ cups water
60 ml/2 fl oz brandy	$\frac{1}{4}$ cup brandy
60 ml/2 fl oz rum	$\frac{1}{4}$ cup rum

Makes 10 glasses

Prick the orange with a skewer about 12 times and place in a saucepan together with the wine, sugar, cloves, allspice, ginger and water. Cover the pan and bring to just below simmering point for 20 minutes (be careful not to boil away the alcohol).

Remove from the heat, add the brandy and rum, pour into a heated punch bowl and serve at once.

LAMB'S WOOL

One of the drinks connected with wassailing, should certainly ensure you're in fine voice fo singing wassailing ditties.

Lamb's Wool was so called because the fluff apple pulp resembles wool.

——METRIC/IMPERIAL—— •	——CUP MEASURES——
4 dessert apples	4 dessert apples
45 ml/3 tbsp water	3 tbsp water
1.2 litres/2 pints brown ale	5 cups brown ale
300 ml/$\frac{1}{2}$ pint sherry	1$\frac{1}{4}$ cups sherry
75 g/3 oz soft brown sugar	$\frac{1}{2}$ cup soft brown suga
5 cm/2 inch piece of cinnamon	2 inch piece of cinnamon
1.25 ml/$\frac{1}{4}$ tsp grated nutmeg	$\frac{1}{4}$ tsp grated nutmeg
1.25 ml/$\frac{1}{4}$ tsp ground ginger	$\frac{1}{4}$ tsp ground ginger
strip of lemon peel	strip of lemon peel

Oven: 350°F/180°C/Mark 4
Makes 8 large glasses

Core the apples and put them into an ove proof dish with the water. Put into the oven ar bake for 20 minutes or until soft. Remove fro the oven, discard the peel and mash the pulp a basin.

Meanwhile, heat the ale, sherry and sugar ir pan, together with the spices and lemon pe• Leave on a very low heat for 20 minutes, th tip into a large, pre-heated punch (or simila bowl. Stir in the hot apple pulp and serve t wassail piping hot.

MULLED WINE

Mulled, or warmed, wine or beer used to be heated quite simply by sticking a red hot poker into the drink, which ensured the alcohol did not evaporate. When heating in a saucepan, make sure not to boil the liquid.

——METRIC/IMPERIAL——	•	——CUP MEASURES——
4 cloves		4 cloves
1 lemon		1 lemon
600 ml/1 pint red wine		2½ cups red wine
75 g/3 oz brown sugar		7 tbsp brown sugar
two 5 cm/2 inch cinnamon sticks		two 2 inch cinnamon sticks
150 ml/¼ pint brandy		⅔ cup brandy

Serves about 4

Push the cloves into the lemon and put in a saucepan with the wine, sugar and cinnamon. Bring to simmering point and simmer gently, covered, for 2–4 minutes. Remove from the heat, add the brandy, strain and serve at once.

Christmas Canapés

Drinks parties are an integral part of the Christmas festivities. A few bite-sized tasty morsels are essential to fend off hunger pangs and inebriety.

PARCELS OF CRAB ON RYE

These vine parcels can be made a day or two ahead and then be kept lightly covered in the refrigerator—don't sit them on their bread discs until the day.

——METRIC/IMPERIAL——	•	——CUP MEASURES——
1 packet vine leaves preserved in brine (containing approx 20–25 leaves)		1 packet grape leaves preserved in brine (containing approx 20–25 leaves)
200 g/7 oz cooked white crab meat		1 cup cooked white crab meat
2 tomatoes		2 medium tomatoes
¼ cucumber		¼ small cucumber
2 spring onions		2 scallions
30 ml/2 level tbsp mayonnaise		2 tbsp mayonnaise
salt and pepper		salt and pepper
45 ml/3 tbsp olive oil		3 tbsp olive oil
15 ml/1 tbsp white wine vinegar		1 tbsp vinegar
pinch dry mustard		pinch dry mustard
1 packet sliced pumpernickel/rye bread—about 250 g/10 oz		1 packet sliced pumpernickel/rye bread—about 10 oz

Makes about 30

Blanch vine leaves in boiling water for 2–3 minutes to soften. Drain and cool. Flake the crab meat, finely dice the skinned and deseeded tomatoes, cucumber and spring onions or scallions. Bind with the mayonnaise and season to taste. Spread the vine leaves out on a flat surface. Halve or quarter the large leaves. Brush lightly with a dressing made from the oil, vinegar, mustard and seasoning all whisked together. Place a 5 ml/1 level tsp /1 tsp crab mixture in the centre of each vine leaf. Fold up neatly, to form small, bite-sized parcels. Place seam-side down on lined trays (non metal), cover with cling film; refrigerate.

Serve each parcel on a square/rectangle of pumpernickel bread.

CHEESE AND PÂTÉ SQUARES

——METRIC/IMPERIAL—— •	——CUP MEASURES——
15 thin slices white bread	15 thin slices white bread
10 large slices dark rye bread	10 large slices dark rye bread
4 eggs, hard-boiled, finely mashed	4 medium eggs, hard-boiled, finely mashed
175 g/6 oz Red Leicester cheese, finely grated	1½ cups finely grated medium Cheddar
about 60 ml/4 tbsp mayonnaise	about 4 tbsp mayonnaise
English mustard powder, to taste	dry mustard, to taste
salt and freshly ground pepper	salt and freshly ground pepper
softened butter, for spreading	softened butter, for spreading
175 g/6 oz fine liver pâté	6 oz fine liver pâté

Makes 60

Cut the crusts off the bread. Place a slice of rye bread on top of a slice of white bread and trim them to the same size. Repeat with remaining slices. Mix eggs and cheese; add enough mayonnaise for a spreading consistency. Add mustard, salt and pepper. Spread one slice of white bread with butter right to the edges. Spread generously with filling, top with a slice of rye. Butter the rye right to the edges, then spread with pâté. Repeat layers once more. Spread one slice of white bread with butter, then place buttered side down on top of pâté filling. Wrap closely in cling film and refrigerate for at least 1 hour. Make four more layered sandwiches in this way, wrapping them in cling film and putting them in the refrigerator as you make them.

Just before serving, unwrap each sandwich and cut into four lengthways. Cut each piece across into three, to make twelve pieces from each sandwich. Arrange on a plate and serve.

CAVIAR MUSHROOMS

——METRIC/IMPERIAL—— •	——CUP MEASURES——
225 g/8 oz even-sized button mushrooms	8 oz even-sized white mushrooms
150 ml/¼ pint soured cream	⅔ cup sour cream
50 g/2 oz jar black Danish-style caviar	2 oz jar black Danish-style caviar
parsley or dill sprigs, to garnish	parsley or dill sprigs, to garnish

Makes about 20

Remove the stalks from the mushrooms and discard. Wipe the mushroom caps with a clean damp cloth. Divide the soured cream between the mushroom caps and spoon a little Danish caviar over each one. Garnish with tiny parsley or dill sprigs. Serve within 30 minutes.

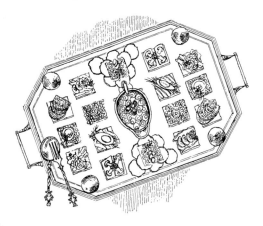

Stocking Fillers

At the start of the twenty-first century it seems impossible to believe that Father Christmas, the present–bringer, has not been with us for ever, but the tradition in Britain is little more than 100 years old–and it came from across the Atlantic Ocean.

Father Christmas *per se* had been around for a long time–a rather amorphous figure, occasionally accompanied by Mother Christmas, who had no specific role and was most frequently depicted looking like Old Father Time, carousing with a glass in his hand.

Meanwhile, in the great melting pot that is the United States, Dutch settlers had brought the tradition of St Nicholas or *Sinterklaas*, and Germans *das Christkind*– later Americanized to Kriss Kringle–who brought presents to children on Christmas Eve.

By 1880 the persona of Santa Claus had been firmly established. Dressed in a red and white robe, with a long, flowing beard, he rode through the sky on a sleigh pulled by reindeer, delivering presents to children on Christmas Eve by climbing down the chimney. With their strong sense of family and love of fairy stories, the Victorians quickly latched on to the idea, but instead of calling him Santa Claus, which was foreign, they gave him a good old English name–Father Christmas.

MITTOON OF PORK

The north of England is the only area where the word mittoon still survives, but mittoons and puptons, both of which closely resemble terrines, were regularly served at the court of Charles II. Sometimes a bread-based forcemeat is spread between the layers of minced or ground pork, but this is rather heavy for modern palates.

METRIC/IMPERIAL	CUP MEASURES
225 g/8 oz belly pork, rind and bone removed	8 oz slab bacon, rind and bone removed
225 g/8 oz chicken livers	8 oz chicken livers
100 g/4 oz fresh white crustless bread	2 cups fresh white crustless bread
225 g/8 oz pork sausagemeat	8 oz bulk sausage
30 ml/2 tbsp juniper berries, crushed	2 tbsp juniper berries, crushed
30 ml/2 tbsp cranberry sauce	2 tbsp cranberry sauce
2.5 ml/$\frac{1}{2}$ tsp grated nutmeg	$\frac{1}{2}$ tsp grated nutmeg
120 ml/8 tbsp brandy	8 tbsp brandy
2 oranges	2 medium oranges
salt and freshly ground pepper	salt and freshly ground pepper
1 egg, beaten	1 medium egg, beaten
450 g/1 lb pork tenderloin	1 lb lean boneless pork
orange slices and whole juniper berries, to garnish	orange slices and whole juniper berries, to garnish

Oven: 325°F/170°C/Mark 3
Serves 8–10

Mince the belly pork or slab bacon with the chicken livers and bread, or work in a food processor. Turn into a bowl, add the sausage meat or bulk sausage, juniper berries, cranberry sauce, nutmeg and half of the brandy. Mix well together. Grate the rind and squeeze the juice of 1 of the oranges. Add to the pâté mixture with salt and pepper to taste, then bind with beaten egg. Put half of the pâté mixture into a greased and base-lined 1 kg/2 lb/7$\frac{1}{2}$ cups loaf tin, pressing it down with the back of the spoon. Cut the pork fillet or lean boneless pork into thin, even slices and arrange over the pâté mixture. Cover with the remaining pâté and press down. Cover the tin with lightly oiled foil. Stand it in a roasting tin half filled with hot water. Bake for 2 hours. Lift the dish out of the water and place heavy weights on top of the foil covering. Leave until cold, then refrigerate for 1–3 days before serving.

To serve, unmould onto a serving plate and wipe away excess fat with absorbent kitchen paper. Squeeze the juice of the remaining orange and pour into a small heavy-based pan. Add the remaining brandy and boil rapidly until reduced. Brush all over the pâté and garnish with orange slices and juniper berries.

> 'Twas the night before Christmas, when all
>   through the house,
> Not a creature was stirring, not even a
>   mouse;
> The stockings were hung by the chimney
>   with care
> In hope that St Nicholas soon would be
>   there.
>
>   Clement C. Moore

Potted Meat

'Potting' was one of the earliest methods of preservation as sealing meat, fish or game with clarified butter (or other fat such as lard or goose grease) prevents bacteria from entering. This makes a potted meat the ideal present as it can be kept for at least a couple of weeks, provided the seal is not broken. Store either in a refrigerator or cold larder.

POTTED PHEASANT

——METRIC/IMPERIAL—— •	——CUP MEASURES——
150 g/5 oz cooked pheasant	5 oz cooked pheasant
50 g/2 oz softened butter	¼ cup/½ stick softened butter
2.5 ml/½ tsp made English mustard	½ tsp hot mustard
5 ml/1 tsp Worcestershire sauce	1 tsp Worcestershire sauce
a good pinch dried thyme	a good pinch dried thyme
meat juices (see method)	meat juices (see method)
salt and freshly milled black pepper	salt and freshly milled black pepper
clarified butter	clarified butter

Serves 6

Either mince the meat finely by hand or in a food processor. Turn into a basin and beat in the softened butter, then the mustard, Worcestershire sauce and thyme.

The addition of meat juices is not essential, but if you have any (do not use a thickened gravy though), beat them in, together with up to about 40 g/1½ oz/3 tbsp of any fat left after cooking the bird.

Season to taste, then pack into a pot. Seal the top with clarified butter. If sealed in this way, the meat will keep for 2 weeks or more. Eat within 2 days once opened.

CUMBERLAND SAUCE

For many years the old ports of Cumberland carried on a thriving trade with the West Indies, so there was always a plentiful supply of rum, brown sugar, spices and citrus fruits. The result is such regional specialities as Cumberland Rum Butter (see page 33), Cumberland Rum Nicky (a sweet tart made with rum and dates) and this sauce, the classic accompaniment for hot ham (see page 21).

——METRIC/IMPERIAL—— •	——CUP MEASURES——
2 oranges	2 medium oranges
2 lemons	2 medium lemons
120 ml/8 level tbsp redcurrant jelly	8 tbsp redcurrant jelly
10 ml/2 tsp mild mustard	2 tsp mild mustard
120 ml/8 tbsp port	8 tbsp port
salt and pepper	salt and pepper
pinch of ground ginger	pinch of ground ginger

Serves 8

Pare the rind thinly from the orange and lemon, free of all the white pith. Cut it in fine strips, cover with water and simmer for 5 minutes. Drain. Squeeze the juice from both fruits. Put the redcurrant jelly, orange juice and lemon juice and mustard in a saucepan and heat gently, stirring, until the jelly dissolves. Simmer for 5 minutes, then add the port. Season with salt and pepper and ginger, if wished.

SPICED APRICOT AND RAISIN CHUTNEY

The perfect accompaniment to cold turkey and ham, chutney came to England from India in the eighteenth century.

——METRIC/IMPERIAL——	•	——CUP MEASURES——
225 g/8 oz dried apricots, soaked overnight		1¼ cups dried apricots, soaked overnight
350 g/12 oz onions, skinned		2 large yellow onions, skinned
finely grated rind and juice of 1 orange		finely grated rind and juice of 1 large orange
1 garlic clove, skinned and crushed		1 garlic clove, skinned and crushed
50 g/2 oz seedless raisins		⅓ cup seedless raisins
225 g/8 oz granulated sugar		1 cup + 2 tbsp sugar
5 ml/1 tsp prepared mustard		1 tsp hot mustard
1.25 ml/¼ tsp ground cinnamon		¼ tsp ground cinnamon
1.25 ml/¼ tsp ground mixed spice		¼ tsp ground mixed spice
5 ml/1 tsp salt		1 tsp salt
450 ml/¾ pint malt vinegar		2 cups malt vinegar

Makes about 1.4 kg/3 lb

Drain the apricots and chop roughly. Discard the water. Chop the onions finely. Place the prepared ingredients in a medium saucepan with the orange rind and juice. Add all the remaining ingredients and bring slowly to the boil. Boil gently, uncovered, stirring occasionally for about 1 hour, or until the chutney is thick, well reduced and no excess liquid remains. Pour into warmed jars, cover with airtight, vinegar-proof tops and label. Store in cool, dry, dark place for 2–3 months to mature before eating.

QUINCE JELLY

——METRIC/IMPERIAL——	•	——CUP MEASURES——
2 kg/4 lb quinces, washed and roughly chopped		4 lb quinces, washed and roughly chopped
3.6 litres/6 pints water		15 cups water
grated rind and juice of 3 lemons		grated rind and juice of 3 lemons
sugar		sugar

Place the fruit in a preserving pan with 2.4 litres 4 pints/10 cups of the water and the lemon rind and juice. Simmer, covered, for 1 hour until the fruit is tender. Stir from time to time to prevent sticking. Spoon the fruit pulp into a jelly bag or cloth attached to the legs of an upturned stool and leave to strain into a large bowl for at least 12 hours.

Return the pulp in the jelly bag to the pan and add the remaining water. Bring to the boil, simmer gently for 30 minutes, then strain again through a jelly bag or cloth for at least 12 hours.

Discard the pulp remaining in the jelly bag. Combine the two lots of extract and measure. Return to the pan with 500 g/1 lb/2¼ cups sugar for each 600 ml/1 pint/2½ cups extract. Heat gently, stirring, until the sugar has dissolved, then boil rapidly for about 10 minutes. Test for a set and, when setting point is reached, take the pan off the heat and remove any scum with a slotted spoon. Pot and cover the jelly.

PICKLED PEARS

It is no coincidence that these pears seem to appear first on tables at Christmas-time each year since, having been made in September or October, they are matured to perfection by then.

METRIC/IMPERIAL	•	CUP MEASURES
900 g/2 lb firm pears, peeled, cored and quartered		2 lb pears, peeled, cored and quartered
450 ml/¾ pint cider vinegar		2 cups cider vinegar
450 ml/1 lb sugar		2¼ cups sugar
1 cinnamon stick		1 cinnamon stick
10 cloves		10 cloves
1 small piece of root ginger		1 small piece of root ginger

Place the pears in a saucepan, cover with boiling water and cook gently for about 5 minutes until almost tender, then drain. Pour the vinegar into a pan and add 300 ml/½ pint water, sugar, cinnamon, cloves and root ginger. Heat gently, stirring, until the sugar has dissolved, then boil for 5 minutes. Add the pears and continue cooking until tender. Remove the pears with a slotted spoon and pack into prepared jars. Strain the vinegar syrup to remove the spices and pour over the pears to cover. Cover the jars immediately with airtight vinegar-proof tops. Store in a cool, dry, dark place for 2–3 months.

FRUIT AND NUT CLUSTERS

Red and green are the classic Christmas colours and the decoration of red and green glacé cherries on these delicious little chocolates carries on the theme. They look enchanting in individual gold or silver sweet cases, if you can get hold of them, but failing that, pack them into a gold or silver box and tie up with red and green ribbon.

METRIC/IMPERIAL	•	CUP MEASURES
100 g/4 oz plain chocolate, broken into small pieces		4 squares semi-sweet chocolate, broken into small pieces
30 ml/2 tbsp clear honey		2 tbsp light honey
100 g/4 oz mixed dried fruit		¾ cup mixed dried fruit
50 g/2 oz chopped nuts, e.g. almonds, hazelnuts or brazils		½ cup chopped nuts, e.g. almonds, hazelnuts or brazils
Decoration		*Decoration*
red and green glacé cherries		red and green candied cherries

Makes 24–28

Place the chocolate and honey in a basin, then either stand this over a pan of hot water until the chocolate has melted, or put into a microwave on low power for 2 minutes. Remove from the heat. Stir in the fruit and nuts until they are well coated with chocolate. Drop teaspoonfuls of the mixture on to waxed paper or non-stick baking parchment or into sweet cases. Press a small piece of red and green glacé/candied cherry into the top of each cluster and leave in a cool place until set.

Mincemeat

Little Jack Horner sat in the corner
Eating a Christmas pie
He put in his thumb and pulled out a plum
And said 'What a good boy am I'

Medieval mincemeat for Christmas pies was just that: minced meat. The meat, usually fat mutton, was cooked with a variety of fruits including prunes (plums), oranges, raisins, dried figs, etc. Over the years the meat content was gradually reduced, so that now it is rarely included at all, though it is usual to add grated or shredded beef suet. However, in the Lake District, pies made with lamb chops and dried

fruits are still popular at Christmas, especiall on the hill farms.

MINCEMEAT

——METRIC/IMPERIAL—— • ——CUP MEASURES——	
1.6 kg/3½ lb dried mixed fruit	9 cups dried mixed fru
225 g/8 oz cooking apples, peeled, cored and grated	1 medium cooking apple, peeled, cored an grated
100 g/4 oz blanched almonds, chopped	1 cup blanched almonds, chopped
450 g/1 lb dark soft brown sugar	2¼ cups soft dark brow sugar
175 g/6 oz shredded beef suet	1½ cups shredded suet
5 ml/1 tsp grated nutmeg	1 tsp grated nutmeg
5 ml/1 tsp ground cinnamon	1 tsp ground cinnamor
grated rind and juice of 1 lemon	grated rind and juice o 1 medium lemon
grated rind and juice of 1 orange	grated rind and juice o 1 medium orange
300 ml/½ pint brandy or sherry	2¼ cups brandy or sher

Makes about 2.5 kg/5½ lb

Put the dried fruits, apples and almonds in large bowl. Add the sugar, suet, spices, lemo and orange rinds and juice and brandy or sherr then mix all the ingredients together thoroughl Cover the mincemeat and leave to stand fc 2 days. Stir well, put into jars and cover. Allo at least 2 weeks to mature before using.

Note For mincemeat that will keep well, use firm, hard type of apple, such as Wellington; juicy apple, such as Bramley's Seedling, ma make the mixture too moist.

GRAND MARNIER TRUFFLES

uring his time as manager of The Savoy in the
90s, César Ritz was approached by a French
dustrialist, who asked his opinion on an orange
queur he had devised. Ritz tasted it and de-
red it excellent—certain (with a little help
om him) to succeed. 'So what shall I call it?'
ked the Frenchman.

Ritz looked at the somewhat self-important
gure of Marnier Lapostolle in front of him.
Vhy Monsieur, call it after yourself, *Le Grand
arnier*.'

Ritz was not to regret this magnanimous
sture. Later, when he wished to open The Ritz
 Paris, he was able to call upon Lapostolle,
hose wealth had been considerably augmented
 Grand Marnier, as a financial backer.

METRIC/IMPERIAL	CUP MEASURES
225 g/8 oz plain chocolate	8 squares semi-sweet chocolate
25 g/1 oz butter	2 tbsp butter
2 egg yolks	2 medium egg yolks
15 ml/1 tbsp Grand Marnier	1 tbsp Grand Marnier
10 ml/2 tsp single cream	2 tsp light cream
drinking chocolate powder or chocolate vermicelli, to decorate	sweetened instant cocoa, to decorate

Makes 24

Break the chocolate in pieces into a heatproof
bowl standing over a saucepan of gently simmering water. Heat gently until the chocolate
has melted, stirring only once or twice after the
chocolate has started to melt. Leave to cool for
about 4 minutes. Beat in the butter, egg yolks,
Grand Marnier and cream and stir until the
mixture is thick. Leave to cool for about 20
minutes, then chill for $1-1\frac{1}{2}$ hours until firm
enough to handle. Form the mixture into small
balls and roll in chocolate powder or vermicelli.
Leave for 1 hour until firm. Arrange the truffles
in sweet cases in a decorative box. Store in the
refrigerator for up to 1 week.

Index